Delille, Edward
Some French writers. Freeport, N.Y., Books for Libraries Press [1972]
221p. 23cm. (Essay index reprint series)

Reprint of the 1893 ed.

1.French literature-19th century-Addresses, essays, lectures. I.Title.

ISBN 0-8369-2543-2 78-37526

SOME FRENCH WRITERS

SOME FRENCH WRITERS

BY

EDWARD DELILLE

Essay Index Reprint Series

BOOKS FOR LIBRARIES PRESS
FREEPORT, NEW YORK

First Published 1893
Reprinted 1972

Library of Congress Cataloging in Publication Data

Delille, Edward.
Some French writers.

(Essay index reprint series)
Reprint of the 1893 ed.
CONTENTS: M. Paul Bourget.--Pierre Loti.--Baudelair
the man. [etc.]
1. French literature--19th century--Addresses, essays, lectures. I. Title.
PQ282.D4 1972 840.9 78-37526
ISBN 0-8369-2543-2

PRINTED IN THE UNITED STATES OF AMERICA
BY
NEW WORLD BOOK MANUFACTURING CO., INC.
HALLANDALE, FLORIDA 33009

CONTENTS.

SOME FRENCH WRITERS.

M. PAUL BOURGET.

I FOUND my way to the top of a winding staircase in the right wing of the *pavillon*, which stood, in the unpretending dignity of its white façade with dark green shutters symmetrically closed, at the back of a graveled courtyard whose gates open on the Rue de Monsieur, calmest among the smaller thoroughfares of the Quartier Saint-Germain. I was admitted into a minute ante-chamber, where the usual sensation of fresh dimness prevailed; was then ushered through a study, hardly less minute, but bright and cheerful in the warm whiteness of its walls and ceiling and rich various hues of many handsomely bound books; some hangings were now drawn aside, and in a subtly-decorated tiny retreat at the back I met Paul Bourget.

A nature of the rarest delicacy and charm—

that was the impression left by this first conversation. Charm is not a thing to be analysed or to be explained; it is a thing simply to be enjoyed. In M. Bourget there are, no doubt, all kinds of complications. Nevertheless, the fact remains that he exercises even upon a stranger the attraction which can only arise from the union of fine brain, ardent spirit, and vivid feeling. What though it be possibly true that, as Verlaine sings, *tout le reste est littérature?*

As Paul Bourget talks, in a voice artistically inflected, one marks how becomingly the soft, abundant dark hair, parted simply at the side, falls over the full, wide, and sufficiently high brow; how the bold yet fine curve of the nose imparts to the entire visage an expression of power; how the round smoothness of the chin denotes a gentleness of nature, and the strongly-marked squareness of the jaw the intensity of the "will to live." The eyes are large, dark, soft, and illumined with a species of confused brightness that lends them their strange expression of mingled melancholy and ardour. It is no doubt from his mountain race of Auvergne that Bourget derives his vein of sentiment, as well as his tenacity of purpose and his enviable acquisitiveness and retentiveness of instinct. The ordinary *enfant de l'Auvergne* will work long, hard, and honestly in order to compass what he would call his "little sack," to which, when once amassed, he will adhere like any limpet. Paul Bourget by not dissimilar methods has built up for himself a fine intellectual fortune, which, instead of dilapidating or frittering away, he guards vigilantly, invests admirably, and unceasingly increases. We all of us, probably, have our particular big man, our favourite great figure in history or in fiction. M. Bourget's big man is understood to be Goethe. This in itself may be a slight indication of character.

Further suggestions of Auvergne are to be found in such a thing as the squareness and sturdiness of the middle-sized, well-knit, open-chested figure. Then for his dress—all Europe by this time knows that M. Bourget is past master in "vestimentary harmony." Such little effects of grace and nicety as may be obtained with the meagre-spread palette of our modern male attire are one and all at his command.

He, with unhesitating hand, has limned for the greater delectation of his readers more than one private figure in contemporary Parisian life. So he cannot justly object if he himself be slightly sketched. The examination of his literary talent is a much more difficult task. His work admits readily of subdivision; he may be considered first as poet, then as critic, and finally as novelist, and then some observations may be added on the general features that distinguish him in the entirety of his endeavour, and that have secured to him his position in the field of literary art.

I.

When he arrived about twenty years ago at man's estate he found himself compelled to give private lessons for a meagre and precarious living. His extreme fondness for literature expressed itself first, as has been often enough the case before him, through the medium of rhyme. But his *Poésies* did not bring him much nearer to the goal of literary fame.

His high-water level in poetry is probably found in "Les Aveux." Yet the sum of the world's harmony would not be very much less had "Les Aveux" remained unwritten. Sighs of desire, gasps of possession, spasms of "sharp" delight and wails of hideous despair; glimpses of nature elaborately dressed-up, here and there a dash or dose of philosophy and metaphysics, and a background in the most approved tone of fleshly pessimism to effectively throw up the whole. The rhythm throughout is supple and caressing. The metres, in their variety, suggest acquaintance with Verlaine, Baudelaire, Gautier, Leconte de Lisle, Sully-Prudhomme, François Coppée, Richepin, and others, to say nothing of *le père à tous*, Hugo. But many lines are strangely weak, and many epithets still weaker.

> " Répéte-toi les vers *célèbres* de Lucrèce "

might be instanced as the acme of *curiosa infelicitas*, were it not for this other gem of M. Bourget's :—

> " Un allegro de Weber, *aussi fin que sublime.*"

And again :—

> " Une mystique intelligence
> L'un vers l'autre nous a conduits,
> Et tu me désirais d'avance
> Dans la détresse de tes nuits."

This, again :—

> " Que reste-t-il de ces heures qui furent miennes,
> *Dis, chère tête aux yeux brûlants*, qu'en reste-t-il ? "

recalls the dialogue in the *Arabian Nights* between a caliph and a speaking head detached from its body.

> " Et les souvenirs se font plus touchants
> *Dans leur volupté qui s'achève en plainte*,"

seems suggestive of feline duos in the night hours. When M. Emile Augier, the famous

French playwright now deceased (but, as Jules Vallès wrote, "La mort n'est pas une excuse"), pronounced his appreciation of the author of *Mensonges*: "Bourget? C'est un cochon triste . . ." he said a thing very mean and very silly, showing that even in Paris the "criticism" of coteries is often mere personal insult. A talent is not to be summed up in two such words. Still, in reading Bourget's verse, even more than his prose, one cannot help perceiving sometimes what Augier had in his mind. "Thou knowest, dear Toby," said Mr. Shandy, "that there is no passion so serious as lust." "Les Aveux" is a little too "serious" here and there. It is the darkness of Baudelaire, without the poignant profundity of tone. "Les femmes ont un art de tout dire sans rien articuler, qui leur permet de parler des plus vilaines choses de ce vilain monde sans y salir la pudeur de leur conversation." Thus M. Bourget himself in *L'Irréparable*. But, although a woman-lover, he has not always followed this good feminine example. His *lapses* herein are all the more to be regretted, that his real note in matters of love and of passion—witness the delicious passages throughout his books, passages heavy with a languorous sweetness as of many hothouse flowers—is one of tenderness and grace; sensuous, indeed, and never rising free from the coils of matter, but yet inclining willingly to adore and to adorn.

> " L'amour naissant est pur comme une piété . . ."

In lines like that, and in pieces like the *romance* which contains this stanza :—

> " Ce temps où tu m'aimas ressemble
> Aux temps charmants, aux temps lointains
> De mon enfance. Ah, gais matins ! . . .
>
> Ah, gais matins ! mon cœur en tremble "—

he comes much nearer to indicating his special shade of amatory sentiment than in the calculating audacities of pieces singing "la chair triste."

The Verlainean treble—or perhaps the strain peculiar to Jean Richepin in some of his earlier *chansons?*—seems well recalled in verses like these :—

> " Et rien n'est plus pareil au soir
> Au soir éteint, au grand soir morne,
> Que la fin d'un sublime espoir,
> De l'espoir d'un bonheur sans borne."

In fact Paul Bourget is never happier than when dealing with the more "intimate" aspects of nature. "Sur l'eau morte du lac de Windermere," he says in his *Etudes et Portraits*, "des îles surgissent, qui ne sont que des mottes de gazon. Le batelier a relevé ses rames, *et la muette beauté des choses est surnaturelle de douceur pénétrante.*" Surely a most delicate and skilful evocation. At his best, in his prose, Bourget has a tenderness of touch which is delightful.

But as a poet, I cannot recognise his right to exist. He is without breadth, without originality, without power.

II.

He says in one of his poems :—

> " Aujourd'hui, si mon cœur tremble je crois qu'il ment ;
> J'ai peur de retrouver dans ses folles extases
> Le souvenir maudit des livres et des phrases."

Not only in love, but in literature, does that " souvenir maudit " haunt him—" moi, l'héritier de tant de livres ici-bas." His poetry is overlaid by literary reminiscence. His novels also groan beneath a burden of book-knowledge. But, in accordance with the universal law of compensation, the self-same quality which has militated against the merit of certain forms of his production has been instrumental in imparting superior excellence to others. " No one knows more, has read more, nor read better, has meditated more profoundly upon what he has read, nor assimilated it more completely." That is what M. Brunetière says of Bourget, and it is true. But so much reading and so much meditation, even when accompanied by great assimilative powers, are not essential to a writer of verse or of fiction. To a philosophic critic, however, they are invaluable; as witness the work done by M. Bourget in that domain which is his stronghold, of literary appreciation allied to semi-scientific thought.

His criticism up to the present has been not very wide in range or considerable in bulk. But for significance, penetration, pregnancy, and perfection of form, it could not easily be surpassed. Two points were perceptible in his earliest successful critiques. First, that his acquaintance with general literature was unusually large, and secondly, that he was familiar with scientific processes of reasoning. Taine, Darwin, and Spencer had given him the notion of an æstho-ethical philosophy having determinism for its motive and induction for its method. From Spinoza, on the other hand, he had learned a system of deduction almost mathematical in its minuteness of detail and precision of final result. He was thus equipped doubly for purposes of ethical and æsthetic speculation. And he used his instruments well. In all points of structure, of mechanism, and, generally speaking, of the perfected, modernised application of means to an end, a critique by M. Bourget was visibly better than anything by his predecessors. They may have been superior in talent or in power. He was superior in treatment and in tone.

A critic may be generated from the decomposition of a poet. This was notably the case with Sainte-Beuve. More frequently the critical faculty will display itself as the temporary expression of a temperament on its way to other things. The latter might perhaps be said of the author of *Essais de Psychologie Contemporaine.* Bourget's firmness of grasp, distinction of feeling, and real or apparent breadth of outlook and depth of thought, spoke of a personality too insistent to remain long content as an interpreter of the literature of other men. The most interesting feature of his criticism was the element it contained of indirect if not unconscious self-revelation. Like charity, the thing began at home. He was explaining his own genius, theories, feelings, and ambitions, through the medium of his comments on the writings and apparent moral nature of men like Baudelaire, Lamartine, de Vigny, Balzac, Amiel, Taine, Renan, Barbey d'Aurevilly, Flaubert, Stendhal, the Goncourt Brothers, and Dumas *fils.* In each and all of these he could discern some tendency, forte, or foible, with which introspection had already rendered him familiar. He was talking, in charming accents and with anxiously chosen words, *about* them, but of himself. The Parisian public was delighted to listen.

Critical method and manner with him are invariable. "Analysis, Psychology, Morals," might be the sub-title to each one of his portraits, studies, and essays. Each *littérateur*, from Flaubert to M. Renan, is taken as the text for a little scientific sermon. "Je suis un moraliste de décadence," he somewhere says. The subject he preaches on most willingly is the disjointedness of an age torn limb from limb by five fashionable fiends, "pessimism," "morbid lust," "excess of analysis," "lack of faith," and the "spirit of dilettanteism."

To study in one's own self the moral and intellectual tendencies of a generation is a system which must evidently be worth exactly as much as the person is who employs it. In M. Bourget's case it has been worth a great deal, and as a critic he stands exceedingly high.

III.

As a novelist the case is different. But Bourget's novels are (like Bourget's nature) interesting no less by reason of their defects than of their qualities; interesting through their mixture of brilliant ingenuity, anxious effort, and slack grace. Ineffectual on the whole, and unoriginal, they yet are attractive and engaging.

The better to understand him as a fiction writer, I should like to retrace his career as a man. From the first, his was a peculiarly reflective mind and impressionable temperament. The horrible things, therefore, which, as he later took occasion to show, must darken life in French colleges till the whole French system of education be reformed, had a precociously disturbing effect upon his spirit. At the time of the Franco-German war he was drawing towards the end of his 'teens, too young to fight, but not too young to taste his share in the cup of France's defeat. Then the episode of the Commune seems especially to have pained him with a sense of the savagery ever latent in humankind. Nor were his private circumstances, as a struggling moneyless young man, of a nature to inspire him with optimism unalloyed. Inhabiting the Latin Quarter, he was enabled to meet and mingle with a few congenial spirits among the poets, painters, and æsthetes who there assemble. But, on the other hand, no doubt he was early made acquainted with the minute trickeries and treacheries, the low, foolish misinterpretation of motives, the mean jealousy and insane intensity of petty spite which so enhance the vexation of existence (supposing these manifestations to be taken seriously in any way) upon certain lower literary levels.

The panorama of Parisian life revolved glittering before his vision. With senses all a-quiver, he drew in at each breath, at each pore, the sights, sounds, odours, colours of the varied, palpitating life around. The pagan air found its way quickly to so delicately organised a brain and slightly turned it. It was perhaps fortunate for Paul Bourget now that his enlightened curiosity urged him to throw off the spell of the Circe among cities sufficiently to travel (if not widely, well) in England, Italy, Greece, and Spain. Meanwhile he fed his mind on Balzac, Flaubert, Stendhal, and the rest. Life he had already studied in coteries and newspaper offices, and a little also in cafés. Eagerly welcomed in salons, he began to study it there.

The first result was *L'Irréparable*. It and the companion tale, *Deuxième Amour*, proved at once beyond question that in M. Bourget, doubtful poet and undoubted critic, a novelist was born into the world. Good or bad? Evidently both. Good at least in the style, always, in Bourget, so charming and seductive; so sweet in its careful caressingness of tone, so rich and subtle in its subdued harmonies of colour and sound. Bad in the conscious imitation of the processes of others; Standhalian dryness of "notation," long Balzacian descriptions of *milieux*. Bad especially in the profusion of details of material luxury: gentlemen who all had their clothes made and their linen washed in London, ladies whose under-garments, dwelt on to the extent of pages, were a delirious dream of baptiste, of lace, and of *mauve* or *couleur pensée* silk. The characters on the whole were indeterminate, drawn loosely, with floating contours. Nor were they exactly human, but seemed rather the more or less vague projections of errant reveries in M. Bourget's mind. There seemed a certain heaviness and thickness, too, about the medium: it was too dense to be transparent. *Mehr licht!* was much wanted in M. Bourget's first romances.

In *Cruelle Enigme*, *André Cornélis*, and *Crime d'Amour* he was at once too lengthily psychological and too freely and abundantly physical. With *Mensonges* he entered (for a time) upon a second and firmer manner. It is interesting and valuable as a study of contemporary Parisian life. It is both vigorous and acute, and may be deemed the masterwork up to now among M. Bourget's romances. *Le Disciple*, unrivalled in its way, is more a metaphysical treatise animated with two or three human figures; *Physiologie de l' Amour Moderne* is psycho-pathology *im*pure and simple, and *Un Cœur de Femme*, Bourget's latest long story, is a return to the weak style of *Crime d'Amour* and *Cruelle Enigme*.

Elements of strength Bourget possesses in his fiction—more than one: closeness and acuteness if not exactly abundance of observation, extraordinary and almost excessive fineness and penetration of analysis, and peculiar charm and sweetness of emotion, with a vein of sentiment sometimes approaching elevation; to say nothing of the richness and suppleness of diction that is a constant quality in his writings, nor of the rare aptitude for philosophic and metaphysical speculation which is probably the master faculty of his mind. The catalogue of shortcomings, on the other hand, contains some formidable items. The sense of action in general is deficient. The characterisation is always literary rather than purely human. And last and worst, humour, the salt of literature as of life, is absent entirely from Paul Bourget's compositions. Wit he has, of a certain intelligently acquired and predeterminedly wrought description; but of humour, absolutely none. For in parts of his books one actually finds him saying, "Go to, I *will* be droll." To what effect, witness the disfigured opening pages of *Le Disciple*.

Altogether, the qualities of his temperament and natural tendencies of his thought better fit him to achieve pre-eminent work in the direction of philosophy, historical and literary criticism, or even pure metaphysics, than to become a master-novelist in his own right—a Balzac, a Flaubert, or a Zola. But of the two *rôles*, which is higher?

IV.

The labours of fifteen or twenty years, from 1872, when first he dabbled in poetic waters, to the present day, when there are so few forms of literary expression that he has left untouched, have placed him in the forefront of literary fame. Letters have done much for him; what precisely has he done for them? And what position may be assigned him among the small group of his compeers and rivals?

Small it undoubtedly is, for in the last analysis

it will be found to comprise but two names—those of Maupassant and Loti. No other French writer of M. Paul Bourget's generation (MM. Daudet, Zola, and others being regarded as representing an earlier day) seems either rare enough or broad enough to be classified with these three. To classify, however, is not enough. One must also try to compare.

To Maupassant a superiority belongs in regard to the faculty of vision. He sees, with eyes hard, insistent, and clear, and, like all who see, can afterwards depict. M. Loti feels rather than sees, but feels how exquisitely well! M. Bourget neither feels like Loti nor sees like Maupassant—he reflects.

The desire and power to reflect is not so much a gift as a tendency. And in literature, if one endure, it can be only by reason of one's gifts. Therefore both Guy de Maupassant with his determined stare and Pierre Loti with his tremulous nerves are "better lives" (to use the insurance agent's phrase) than is M. Bourget with his highly-organised brain. Yet the possession of such a brain implies, almost as a necessity, the exercise of invaluable qualities of taste, comprehension, and subsequent explication. Through these M. Bourget, psychologist, feminist, cosmopolite, and man of semi-philosophic leanings and completely literary culture, will have had a salutary influence upon the whole on contemporary French letters, if only through the part he has played in contributing to redeem them from the naturalistic slough.

A born critic, consequently no creator. A mere dexterous, brilliant, successful representative of the minor species "homme de lettres." But most assuredly he is welcomed. And now, *l'Académie l'attend.*

PIERRE LOTI.

I.

TOTALLY unknown one day, on the next he had brought out a romance and was famous. It was kind of M. Brunetière to praise him—albeit a little gingerly and a long time after his initial success—but no doubt M. Loti thought it still kinder of the French and European public to welcome him with open arms from his *début*, entering into no subtle distinctions as to whether he isn't too much of an artist to be a genius, but simply acclaiming him as one of the most charming and admirable writers of this or any time. Such a triumph must have been all the more delightful for its spontaneity. How rare that an author should give all but his full measure at his first attempt, and rarer that readers should recognise him at once for what he is! No other French writer of the day can claim to have succeeded so quickly.

There are reasons for every literary success—even that of a Montépin or a G. R. Sims. The reasons for M. Loti's success are, to my way of thinking, twofold.

First, his "non-professionalism" was a particular point in his favour. For a good many years past in France it has been felt that fiction was assuming the character of a mechanical product. So much of art was there in these latter-day *chefs-d'œuvre*, that hardly any room remained for life, heart, or soul. George Sand, Dumas *père*, and Balzac were inartistic, but pre-eminently intuitive and inspired. MM. Flaubert, De Goncourt, Daudet, Zola wrote and composed with much more science and skill, but beneath the new literature's admirably planed and polished and most curiously inlaid and ornamented surface there lurked a dissatisfying void. Would no modern writer arise who, whilst possessing at least a tincture of the Flaubert-Goncourt art, should yet treat fiction less as a means of displaying his cunning of hand than of expressing his state and tendencies of soul? Hereupon emerged M. Loti, and the anxious problem was solved. With his instinctive deftness of handling he more than satisfied the demands of even the greatest sticklers for "l'écriture." But evidently art *per se* was less a primary than a subsidiary consideration in the case of this young naval officer who is engaged from one year's end to another in circumnavigating the globe, and remains consequently foreign to the spirit of the coteries. The public, probably, did not go into the question with this degree of minuteness. They were conscious, however, of a novel state of feeling on the part of the new author; and this in itself was enough to make Pierre Loti welcome.

Then the exotic, outlandish element in Loti acted as a more powerful charm on French readers than would have been the case with any others. It came, in the French literature of the day, not only as a rarity but as a relief. French literature has long been centralised, like every other good or bad thing French. Writers of talent and sometimes indeed genius have devoted their whole powers to the study of the metropolis solely, and, within that metropolis, have sought out mainly the spots of most consummate disease and decay.

It has been Paris only, Paris ever, throughout a long series of enormously able, intensely elaborated literary works for quite a couple of generations. The atmosphere of French letters had become thick and slab with Paris, and it was high time some one should throw wide a casement, letting into all this stew and closeness, as of a long-shut over-heated room, the breath and murmurs of the world without. That some one has been Pierre Loti. Small wonder if the wizard worked such enchantment with one wave of his wand.

II.

Full of all passion, all beauty, all charm; full also of grief, bewilderment, and pain, is the strange, wild, various land—a land comprising many lands—whereunto the magician transports us. Most potent, most peculiar the spells he weaves. We are in the East, upon the banks of the Bosphorus: through the devious crowded streets of Constantinople we wander, or else plunge deep into the sights and sounds of the dim bazaars. We stand gazing upon the water thick with barques, at the hour when the sun sinks forlorn amidst farewell sanguineous splendours—the sun of Baudelaire's divine *Harmonie du Soir*:—

"Le soleil s'est noyé dans son sang qui se fige . . ."

until darkness, studded with stars, begins to ascend the skies. By degrees a sense of weirdness, of mystery, arises, and at once oppresses and excites us. Passing presently, when night has fallen, through the burial-ground choked up with nameless tombs, a penetrating chill will creep upon us—an apprehension, thrilling in its acuteness, of the ceaseless, unrestrainable flux of things, the littleness of life and sombre greatness of death. Meanwhile, in her chamber hung with draperies, the Turkish maid Aziyadé awaits the Frank, her lover. The scene changes. We are on an island in Polynesia with Rarahu among the groves of palms. The air is fervid and fragrant; nature all round us breathes a startling, savage charm. "In the spell of Tahiti there is something of the weird sadness which hangs over all these Oceanic isles—their isolation in the vast, far-off Pacific—the sea-wind—the moan of the breakers—the density of shade—the hoarse, melancholy voices of the islanders, who wander, singing, amid the trunks of the cocoa-palms, which are so amazingly tall, and white, and slender." And Rarahu, "the little arum-flower," her dusky visage crowned with black silken tresses, and illumined by the bright softness of the great eyes—those eyes, set so near together beneath the brow, that "when she was laughing and gay, they gave her face the mischievous shyness of a marmoset's:" Rarahu, "scarcely responsible for the aberrations of her strangely ardent and vehement nature," poor descendant of a doomed, dwindling race, who, when she loved, loved too well! "All that the purest and most heartbroken affection, the most boundless devotion can suggest to the soul of a passionate little creature of fifteen, she poured forth in her Maori tongue, with wild extravagance and the strangest imagery." Poor Rarahu! Her fate, like that of most things delicate and lovely, is to be broken, to decline and die:—

> "Alas! alas! the little arum flower was once so pretty!
> Alas! alas! now it is faded. . . ."

Again the scene changes, shifting to Africa, to Bled-el-Ateuch, the "land of thirst." That private of the *Spahis*, in his Turkish cap with drooping tassel and crimson cloak with ample folds, is Jean Peyral, simple as a boy, though stalwart as a man. In the distant mountain village in France, the honest old mother and the faithful sweetheart have year by year been looking, sorely anxious, for the young *spahi's* return. But the black spell of Africa has fallen upon him, and he lingers in Bled-el-Ateuch. After long but useless struggles he now lives only for the negress Fatou-gaye. She twined her thin arms about him, and the flitting bats at eventide were witnesses to their first embrace of love. Down, down Jean sank in a pool of dark oblivion.

Pretty she was, with her bead-like eyes, her enigmatic smile, and head completely shaven but for those five little twisted locks. Pretty and, though black, yet human. And he was melancholy and alone. A dreary land, too, this of the "Ateuch" or "great thirst." On the forlorn coast where Jean first landed is heard eternally "la plainte des brisants d'Afrique." Farther inwards are the villages, the "stations," with their uncouth houses and huts. And all round these and beyond—the great, hot, white, lonely, mournful plains, where only dead herbage bespeckles the soil, with here and there the meagreness of a palm, or else one of those "colossal baobab-trees, which are like the mastodons of the vegetable kingdom, whose naked branches are inhabited by families of vultures, lizards, and bats." The slightest details of the slightest things are strange—the ants are white, the birds pink, the lizards blue. In the tepid waters of the streams, beneath the shade of singular growths, the great grey crocodiles doze and dream, their jaws opening and shutting as though in their slumbers they imagined they were seizing a prey; while crabs, with a single ivory-white claw, move restlessly and viciously to and fro. At night-time "the dog-star rises, the moon is in the zenith, the silence so deep that a listener is touched with dread. On the pink sands the tall euphorbias show bluish beneath the gleams of the moon; the shadows they cast are short and hard, and the outline of even the smallest objects is reflected with a kind of glacial sharpness. It is a scene fraught with lifelessness and mystery." Sometimes, too, through the darkness, will be heard the shouts of the savages at their lust-dance, too hideous to be described: "To a crazy rhythm, to notes such as might be struck by a madman, they all yell together, as they leap high into the air: '*Anamalis fobil! faramata hi!*'" . . . Yet another savage song is Jean the *spahi* destined to hear in these burning wastes—the song of death, which to him means deliverance from degradation and Fatou-gaye; the song of the final delirium, as, alone and helpless amid the brush of the parched plain, he lies, his chest tortured with a great wound, and before his glazing eyes the semblance, and within his throbbing ear something similar to the sound, of a string of black men mystically circling, and at intervals calling: "*Djean! Djean!* come and join us in our round:" the vast round, never-ending, which nothing human may evade. Meanwhile, the mother and the sweetheart on the Vosgesian slope still wait and weep as the weeks and months roll by, with no news from the absent truant son. The great black land has devoured him. They will see their Jean no more.—Again Africa, but now, Morocco, at the heart of the most intensely Mohammedan of empires. Here the winding-sheet of Islam covers all. The very sounds of the Arabian bagpipe, as they shrill upon the ear at Tangiers from beneath the balcony of the banal modern hotel, seem as it were a hymn in celebration of the spirit of remote antiquity brooding everywhere but on the merest fringes of this land. Farther inwards, an April green is upon the hills and fields. In all the broad, undulating distance, nothing human to be seen save occasionally some shepherd, a little motionless heap of grey garments—his sheep or cattle, mere dots, wide-scattered. At the different towns upon the way, gorgeous cavalcades in honour of these Europeans on their mission to the town of Fez. Fez itself, ancient legendary stronghold of Mohammedanism on African soil. Its great white buildings, so closely pent within the narrow, ill-kept streets, are crumbling like the Empire which Fez represents. The hawk-like Sultan, half-warrior, half-sage, and all fanatic, appears a figure from some by-gone age as he advances, with cumbrous barbaric pomp and state of attendants and officials, into the middle of the vast court-yard of his palace, so vast that the monarch in the centre looks scarcely bigger than a fly upon the expanse of a pane. And now the return to and arrival at the modernised capital upon the coast. Heavy-featured English girls in straw hats and brown leather shoes; German waiters in the principal hotels; gas, and, in a word, the thing which we call "civilization." Cannot one comprehend and almost share the sentiments thus expressed by the explorer :—" Personellement j'avoue que j'aimerais mieux être le très saint calife que de présider le plus parlementaire, la plus lettrée, la plus industrieuse des républiques ? "—Now, the coast of north-eastern China. Thick-ribbed ice far out into the bay; black heavy clouds overspreading the fierce sky, and upon all things a spell of deep, dead silence, as though Nature, in dreary muteness, were awaiting the return of Chaos and Universal Night. . . . The travellers disembark, and are whirled inland by a native conveyance which groans and quivers as it rolls. Mile after mile through the bitter air, upon the hardness of the frozen soil, amid scenes so swiftly shifting and peculiar and unwonted, that the brain is scarce able to control the impressions made upon the nerves by the bewildered senses, and the entire being seems to mingle with and be lost in the succession of surrounding sights and sounds: "Our mind seems to be merged in the clouds of dust and in the driver's ta! ta! ta!; it seems to pass into the jangling of the bells, the bumping of the waggon, the creeking of the wheels in every rut, the howls of the wind which is blowing with fury." Tartars stare stolidly out of their small sidelong eyes. The little rough-coated native horses squeal and prance. Now is caught up, and rapidly left behind, a string of patient, plodding camels, with the severe, stupid, resigned expression of their profile. Far off upon the wide-spread plain, scores and scores of minute canals lie glittering, like steel needles tossed down from heaven by a giant's hand. And now houses, full of a babel of strange sounds from metallic Mongolian throats, as, alighting, the travellers fight their way towards a room. And now, again, great towns, with the infinitude of their outlandish characteristics.—The next change is to Japan: "Nagasaki, as yet unseen, lies at the extremity of this long and curious bay. All around us was admirably green. The strong sea-breeze had suddenly fallen, and was succeeded by a perfect calm; the atmosphere, now very warm, was laden with the perfume of flowers. In the valley resounded the ceaseless whirr of the cicalas, answering each other from one shore to another; the mountains re-echoed with innumerable sounds; the whole country seemed to vibrate like crystal. On our way we passed among myriads of Japanese junks gliding softly, wafted by imperceptible breezes, on the unruffled water; their motion could scarcely be heard, and their white sails, stretched out on yards, fell languidly in a thousand horizontal folds like window-blinds, their strangely contorted poops, rising castlewise in the air, reminding one of the towering ships of the Middle Ages. In the midst of the intense greenery of this wall of mountains, they stood out with a snowy whiteness." Japan, the land of temples, of dwarf trees, of orchards that are oceans of bloom; the land of houses with white paper panels, big mountains, and little *mousmés* like "Madame Chrysanthème;" *mousmés* with droll little manners, but apparently not much cumbered with soul. Passionless indeed and pallid, is Chrysanthème by the side of her sisters in "exotism," Aziyadé, Fatou-gaye, and Rarahu.

To many other parts of the globe does our wizard convoke us. To the Montenegrin mountains with Pasquala Ivanovitch the shepherdess, grey-eyed and yellow-haired. To Herzegovina, where a river, the Trebinitza ("old Styx must have looked like it") flows over a stony bed amid the expanse of a stony plain. "As though there were a curse upon it, nothing will grow upon its banks." To Algiers, where the "three ladies of the Kasbah," painted, perfumed, and peering after nightfall with an occasional subdued hiss through the grating in the big door of their gloomy dwelling in that uphill street of the "old town," lead their life of dead torpor by day and, during nocturnal hours, of secret mercenary sin. To the sand-wastes of the East African shore, where the Somalis wander seeking whom they may devour. To Tonquin, where Frenchmen fight, and fall, and if captured, are put lingeringly to death.

But within no spot of ground does the spell work so strongly as within the magician's own native land. Brittany, home of sailors, of fishermen, and of their parents, sweethearts, children, and wives: of Yves, of Yann, of Sylvestre, of Marie, she who loved and suffered and yet was happy at last, of Marguerite or "Gaud," whose young life so soon was crushed by grief; Brittany, melancholy primitive land of an ancient race, an ancient speech, an ardent faith, granite land opposing the barrier of its projecting coast against the assaults and perennial encroachments of the sea. At times so furious, that sea, at times again so gentle—does it not seem, on the calm summer evenings when it rests from its winter's rages, as though it were crooning a kind of dirge?

> "Où sont-ils, les marins perdus dans les nuits noires?
> O flots, que vous savez de lugubres histoires,
> Flots profonds redoutés des mères à genoux!
> Vous vous les racontez en montant les marées,
> Et c'est ce qui vous fait ces voix si désolées
> Que vous avez le soir, quand vous venez vers nous."

III.

Upon inquiring more nearly into Loti's methods and results, it becomes at once apparent that simplicity of tone and directness of address are the chief characteristics of his manner. Hereby he gains a happy fluidity and ease, contrasting with the hard strenuousness of other modern French stylists. M. Barrès has qualified Loti as being *violemment sensuel.* This at first sight may appear questionable as an explanation of Loti's art. A moment's thought, however, will show the judgment involved to be correct. It is just this intensity of M. Loti's sensuous, physical impressions (and how fortunate for him and us that circumstances should have placed him among precisely the conditions of environment and experience best calculated to excite them to the utmost!) which, quite simply and naturally, finds its expression in words and phrases of corresponding intensity. Given certain states of vision and feeling, and what follows logically is—*Aziyadé, Le Mariage de Loti, Le Roman d'un Spahi, Mon Frère Yves, Madame Chrysanthème, Pêcheur d'Islande.* "Simply and naturally," however, are not perhaps just terms to be used in this connection. Art is never simple, never natural, but always difficult and complex. It must appear natural and simple, else it remains imperfect; *ars celare* must always be last and greatest. The tendency towards art—perhaps even artifice—is very strong with M. Loti. But at bottom what is this tendency, save the desire for the most exact attainable expression of one's thought or feeling? Art cultivated as a means and not an end proves in the long run a generous mistress, and thus it is that Pierre Loti has progressed within not many years from the comparative smallness of a production like *Aziyadé* to the breadth and largeness of *Pêcheur d'Islande*—from a statuette, albeit of silver, to a statue.

True, in great degree he found his art ready fashioned to his hand. During the past fifty years in France the protracted endeavours of a series of marvellous stylists—Hugo, Flaubert, the Goncourts, Gautier, Baudelaire, Daudet even—have had the effect of transforming the French tongue from one of the poorest into one of the richest instruments of expression; from one of the hardest and stiffest, into one of the subtlest and most supple. The meagre, rigid forms of "classicism" have been superseded by the vivid, rapid turns, the spontaneous, evocatory indications, the active limber nakedness as it were, characterising French style as the best artists write it to-day. Loti was all the readier to resort to the novel medium, that it really is the medium in which he feels and thinks. His emotion (and he is all emotion) is either, so to speak, in spurts, that "write themselves" as of their own accord in those little, vibrant, condensed, elliptical phrases, or else is in shades so exquisite and delicate, that but for the acutely sensitive selection of adjective and of verb, they could not possibly be fixed.

Here I will string together a number of passages from Loti at large. The selection is not much more rationally critical than that of the Indian who decks himself promiscuously with feathers and beads. But I shall claim indulgence for my system of citations, as going some way in exemplification of certain points discussed above.

. . . The melancholy of the exiled *spahi* in

Senegambia, indicated — so subtly! — by this quivering simplicity of phrase :—

> " Le soleil couché, la nuit tomba, *et ses idées s'en allèrent tout à fait au triste.*"

The rustic pathos of the mother's letter to her soldier son :—

> " Ton père dit qu'il en a vu de rudes pour les jeunes gens qui ne sont pas bien raisonnables, par rapport à des camarades qui les entraînent à la boisson et à de méchantes femmes qui se tiennent là exprès pour les faire tomber dans le mal."

The mingled feeling and music of this small phrase, soft and gentle as a maiden's kiss :—

> " Les colibris chantaient de leur toute petite voix douce, pareille à la voix d'hirondelles qui jaseraient en sourdine."

Then the graceful humour and kindliness of the allusions to animals, the smallest and frailest among which are most interesting, apparently, in the eyes of the author :—

> " Une tortue, drôle à force d'être petite, *un atôme de tortue.*"
>
> " Le perroquet d'Yves,—son perroquet était un hibou. Il y a de bizarres destinées sur la terre, ainsi celle de ce hibou faisant le tour du monde en haut d'un mâit. Quel sort inattendu ! "

Now, these effects of "cosmic" desolation :—

"Des conceptions ténébreuses, pleines de mystère, comme des traces d'une existence antérieure à celle de ce monde."

"Tout est fondu, le ciel et les eaux, dans des profondeurs cosmiques, vagues, infinies."

"Mais c'était une lumière pâle, pâle, qui ne ressemblait à rien; elle traînait sur les choses comme des reflets de soleil mort."

This little sheaf of reflections, pessimistic, philosophical, and moral, of a kind frequent enough in the works of Pierre Loti :—

"Il y a en nous un tas d'individus différents, sans compter les animaux."

"A l'état sauvage, la beauté physique est incompatible avec la laideur morale."

"Parce que nous avons rendu par une forme concise quelque chose d'inintelligible, le comprenons-nous mieux pour ça ?"

Here, a passage in Loti's peculiar vein of satire; not much more than a half-dozen words, and yet how vivid the effect :—

"Des femmes avec beaucoup de fleurs fausses sur des têtes communes."

Now, one of Loti's many seascapes :—

"La grande houle, presque éternelle dans ces régions, était molle, et s'en allait en mourant. C'étaient de longues montagnes d'eau, aux formes douces et arrondies, pareilles à des ondulations lourdes de mercure, ou à des coulées de métal qui se refroidissent."

Then, for their synthetic force, these touches :—

"Au moral comme au physique, grand, fort et beau, avec quelques irrégularités de détails."

"Nous étions des enfants alors—aujourd'hui des hommes faits—demain . . . la vieillesse—après-demain, mourir."

"Des mendiants qui avaient des cheveux gris sur des têtes vides n'ayant jamais rien contenu."

A corpse, decaying at the bottom of the sea :—

"Il va passer dans les plantes de pierre qui n'ont pas de couleur, dans les bêtes lentes qui sont sans forme et sans yeux."

Again, the deep, pathetic humanity of this. The old peasant-woman has received official notification of the death in far-off lands of the grandson she so cherished, and, as she hastens homeward along the stony, interminable road—

"Elle s'efforçait de ne pas *trop bien comprendre.*"

In their hut two solitary women, one old, the other young, but both unhappy, humble, and poor, sit at their scanty evening meal :—

"Elles soupaient sur une table presque informe à force d'être usée, mais encore épaisse comme le tronc d'un gros chêne. Et le grillon ne manquait jamais de leur recommencer sa petite musique à son d'argent."

A woman's despair, thus simply denoted :—

"Alors la chaumière lui sembla plus désolée, la misère plus dure, le monde plus vide—et elle baissa la tête avec une envie de mourir."

The mysterious charm of female lips :—

"Elle a ces lèvres aux contours fins et fermes, aux coins très profonds, qui sont souvent toute la beauté attirante et mortelle d'un visage de femme."

Now—in English, alas!—Yves and his certificate-book :—

"Here are the early years when he earned fifteen francs a month, and kept ten to give to his mother; years which he passed with the wind blowing full on his chest, living half-naked in the tops of those mighty oscillating stems which serve as masts, wandering without a care in his mind over the everchanging waste of waters; then come restless years, when the passions of youth dawn and assume tangible form in the inexperienced mind, becoming realised by-and-bye in brutish boozings or in dreams of touching purity, according to the character of the places to which the wind wafts him, or that of the woman upon whom he happens to light, terrible awakenings of the heart and senses, great outbursts, followed by a return to the ascetic life of the ocean, immured in a floating cloister: all these things lie indicated beneath the numbers, names, and dates, which are accumulating, year by year, on a poor sailor's certificate-book. These yellow leaves contain a strange poem of adventures and sufferings."

And from *Pêcheur d'Islande*, Gaud watching, as it

melts gradually into the horizon, the barque that bears away from her Yann, her husband, whom she is never to see again :—

"As the *Léopoldine* receded beyond the line of vision, Gaud, as if drawn by a magnet, followed the pathway all along the cliffs till where she had to stop, because the land came to an end; she then sat down at the foot of a tall cross, which rises amidst the gorse and stones. As it was rather an elevated spot, the sea, as seen from there, appeared to be rimmed, as in a bowl, and the *Léopoldine*, now a mere dot, appeared sailing up the incline of that immense circle. The water rose in great, slow undulations; but over the great space where Yann still was, all seemed calm.

"Gaud still gazed at the ship, trying to fix its image well in her brain, so that she might recognise it again from afar, when she should return to the same place to watch for its home-coming."

IV.

Were it a question of naming Loti's masterpiece, probably the choice of the majority of readers would fall on *Pêcheur d'Islande.* Some may—and do—prefer the subtler and more singular and artificial charm of the smaller books, such as *Le Roman d'un Spahi* and *Le Mariage de Loti;* others there are whom the picturesqueness of *Mon Frère Yves* more particularly attracts; but none, I should imagine, can fail to recognise that in the larger breadth of its proportions, greater depth and sanity of its tone, and superior simplicity of its treatment, *Pêcheur d'Islande*, among the little group of Pierre Loti's works stands alone. The others may be regarded as dainty, delicious aquarelles or pastels; this is a canvas, swept with bolder brush. There is a touch of the epic spirit in *Pêcheur d'Islande*, and, indeed, the book itself might almost be termed an epic—the Epic of the Sea. Surely no one has depicted, or rather personified, the ocean's hundred moods of storm and calm with so masterly, so magical a hand. We seem to live with the great, weird, cosmic life of the billows as they heave beneath the lashing of the wind; or as they melt away in long undulations at the numbing touch of northern mists; or again, as they sink quietly into a million minute ripples, touched with gold by the tropical sun. At every chapter in *Pêcheur d'Islande* the Ocean sings its varying chorus to the drama of human passions and woes.

A great writer Loti is not; an admirable writer he is. Of course his merits are not without their corresponding defects. The tremulous refinement of his sensibilities can degenerate into something very like hysteria. The delicate tenderness of his emotion occasionally becomes lachrymose. And last and worst, the troubled ardour of his passion verges dangerously upon disease. One can discern all this clearly enough, but one isn't careful to enlarge upon the theme. Why fasten and feed upon the unsound spots of a genius, if one belong not to the school of critical ghouls?

BAUDELAIRE; THE MAN.

> "Nous traînions tristement nos ennuis, accroupis
> Et voûtés sous le ciel carré des solitudes
> Où l'enfant boit, dix ans, l'âpre lait des études."

Thus sang Baudelaire in his earliest piece. His college days, evidently, were no "happy seed-time" for the author of the *Fleurs du Mal.*

Next came those six months which Baudelaire spent in the East, and which coloured so profoundly and for all the rest of his life his thought, feeling, and consequently verse. None of Baudelaire's later associates could ever learn the exact truth concerning this mysterious voyage; for Baudelaire was one of those who "embroider." Other people, of the kind who couldn't embroider if they would, are eager to denounce them as liars. Liars they are not—but, it may be, persons who dislike the bare simplicity of the letter.

According to one critic, a profound instability was the chief moral characteristic of Charles

Baudelaire. It should, however, be remembered that none found Baudelaire more "unstable" than did Baudelaire himself to his undoing. Why must a man be hated, despised, and denounced because—doing nobody else any harm—he is what people denominate "his own enemy"? Isn't it enough to err and to suffer, without being also pharisaically damned? Baudelaire's charlatan fondness for singularity in dress, speech, and manner is also one of the battle-horses of the anti-Baudelaireans. No doubt a dash of charlatanism was a necessary ingredient of Baudelaire's temperament, without which we should not now have his art.

Untrustworthy he may have been, but likewise charming, seductive, interesting in an extraordinary degree. And never more so than on his first coming to Paris, as a returned Oriental traveller, a critic, a poet, a dandy, and a capitalist, just turned twenty-one. He was of a good height and had a lithe feline figure. His high white brow, searching luminous brown eyes, nose of noticeable size and shape (*nez de priseur*, he called it, with the open palpitating nostril, sure mark of pride if not of power), lip at once sensual and sensitive, chin short, somewhat rounded, and stamped with the central cleft denoting amiability akin to weakness, and jaw—a feline jaw—

strong, square, and large: all these were features composing a countenance more than handsome, singular.

Brummel's principles of attire were Baudelaire's, for just so long as Baudelaire could afford fine raiment. In garments of sober hue and anxious rectitude of cut, with snow-white linen and glittering lacquered boots, he was often to be seen in the old brooding torpid streets within sound of the bells of Notre-Dame half-a-century ago. In his hotel-rooms in the Latin Quarter (he had always, by the way, a strange fancy for living as high up towards the tops of houses as he could get) at first he caused the lower panes of his windows to be ground, so that he might be relieved from the view of adjacent roofs and upper storeys. Soon, however, no aspect of the life of towns was unwelcome to the spirit of the author of the *Fleurs du Mal*. He came in an age when all is artificial, amid a state of society which from top to bottom is artifice, recalling nothing so much as those agglomerations of tables and chairs maintained in equilibrium by Japanese jugglers upon the extreme tip of their nose. He himself wrote: "Le monde ne marche que par le malentendu. . . . C'est par le malentendu universel que tout le monde s'accorde." So that he, too, should be artificial, was but natural.

Through the force of exterior circumstances, a sentence was passed on him of artificiality for life. He could not have helped being artificial, had he ever so much desired. And thus it is that we find him falling under the apparently puerile spell of dandyism; thus, that we see him experimenting upon some of the most recondite varieties of sensation; thus, that we perceive him seeking and finding the deep poetic interest which underlies existence in great towns, as distinguished from the "idyllism" of fields and hills; and thus, finally, that we find him elaborating some of the most bizarrely beautiful and most singularly, strangely significant verse and poetic prose.

Baudelaire, personally as well as poetically, had the peculiar seductiveness of the complex—of that which some might call the false. The account in Gautier's famous sketch of Baudelaire's careful, measured diction, in conversation scarcely less chastened than in writing, with the secret suggestive emphasis laid upon particular syllables and words, is interesting as characteristic of the man. The subtle magic enclosed in words, viewed apart from their sense and merely as collocations of letters, must early have been disclosed to a sense of such acuteness and a taste of such delicacy as were his. Then the peculiar mode of enunciation, whereby each piece becomes in a manner assimilated to a musical composition: that would have been invented by him had he not found it in the atmosphere of his time, and on the lips of men like Gautier and Hugo. Baudelaire's own verse is not melodious,—it is harmonic; as much finer and rarer than mere verbal music, as harmony is more powerful and profound than melody. How intense, for example, is the harmony here:—

"O douleur! ô douleur! le Temps mange la vie,
Et l'obscur Ennemi qui nous ronge le cœur
Du sang que nous perdons croît et se fortifie!"

And again:—

"Pouvons-nous étouffer le vieux, le long Remords
Qui vit, s'agite et se tortille,
Et se nourrit de nous comme le ver des morts,
Comme du chêne la chenille?
Pouvons-nous étouffer l'implacable Remords?"

Again:—

"Ma Douleur, donne-moi la main; viens par ici
Loin d'eux; vois se pencher les défuntes Années
Sur les balcons du ciel, en robes surannées;
Surgir du fond des eaux le Regret soupirant;
Le soleil moribond s'endormir sous une arche,
Et comme un long linceul traînant à l'orient,
Entends, ma chère, entends la douce Nuit qui marche."

And, to my taste, finer still:—

"J'ai vu parfois au fond d'un théâtre banal
Qu'enflammait l'orchestre sonore,
Une fée allumer dans un ciel infernal
Une miraculeuse aurore;
J'ai vu parfois au fond d'un théatre banal

"Un être, qui n'était que lumière, or et gaze,
Terrasser l'énorme Satan;
Mais mon cœur que jamais ne visite l'extase.
Est un théâtre où l'on attend
Toujours, toujours en vain l'Etre aux ailes de gaze."

Is there not, herein, a resonance as of bronze smitten and vibrating, together with the density of substance, definiteness of contour, smoothness of surface, brilliancy of polish, and sombre richness of hue which distinguish some admirable antique? Rigid perfection of form, thrilling significance of tone, are the twin qualities of all Charles Baudelaire's best art.

One can see him and hear him intoning a piece like his "Mendiante Rousse" for the benefit of a circle of youthful poets like his friends Prarond, Levavasseur, and others in a room at that celebrated Hôtel Pimodan, where Gautier afterwards dwelt. They eyed Baudelaire a little askance, did these worthy young *littérateurs*, whose names now never occur save perchance in connection with his. They deemed him "singular"—as probably he was, seeing what the proportion is of men of genius amongst the mass of humankind.

So much has been said and written concerning Baudelaire's bad traits—supposed or real—that something ought in fairness to be said concerning his undoubtedly good qualities. He was an ardent admirer and a most devoted friend. From the first he was a worshipper of Hugo, Gautier, Balzac, Banville, Flaubert, Stendhal and Leconte de Lisle. To Delacroix:—

> "Delacroix, lac de sang hanté des mauvais anges . . ."

he was loyal throughout the painter's life and after his death. Wagner he fairly discovered; speaking with regard to Paris, where at that time the German Titan was being laughed and whistled off the stage. Then Sainte-Beuve. Baudelaire placed him upon a pedestal, whereas Sainte-Beuve, the smaller of the two both in powers and in feeling, viewed Baudelaire always rather doubtfully, according to his tendency in most things and regarding most people. Gautier could truly write of Baudelaire: "Ce poète avait l'amour et l'admiration au plus haut degré."

In behalf of how many writers, poets, painters,

draughtsmen of his day, did Baudelaire manifest the vivacity of his sympathies and the unerringness of his appreciation? Pétrus Borel, Paul Dupont, Barbier, Mürger, Marceline Desbordes-Valmore, Daumier, Corot, Manet, and a score of others (to say nothing of Edgar Poe, whom Baudelaire, according to his early promise, succeeded in rendering "un grand homme pour la France"): all these he brought into light and notice through the medium of perhaps the most admirable literary criticism yet known.

It should be noted, moreover, that Baudelaire was not attracted only towards what is distinguished, fine and grand. That which is too delicate, too rare, too slight and tender to stand much chance of winning the material prizes of success, appealed with no less force to his spirit. "Le poète se sent irrésistiblement entraîné vers tout ce qui est faible, ruiné, contristé, orphelin." Only the contentedly mediocre, the complacently vulgar, did Baudelaire violently detest and denounce. In this doubtless he was wrong. For even mediocrity, even vulgarity, even Philistinism are human.

That, possessing his critical powers, Baudelaire should not have secured for himself the profits and prestige of the authoritative critic—that he should not, for instance, have rivalled and surpassed herein his lukewarm friend Sainte-Beuve—appears at first sight unaccountable. Baudelaire's *Art Romantique*, that collection of the most searching and suggestive, most brilliant yet solid studies in the very best literature of his day; his *Salons* and other articles on painting (as far superior to Diderot's *Salons* as diamonds to cut glass) place beyond doubt, though they form hardly the matter of a volume, the fact that Baudelaire was the keenest *esthéticien* of the century in France. But the explanation of Baudelaire's comparative inefficacy in professional spheres of criticism must be sought for in his devotion to the pure poetic principle. Baudelaire's verse was exacting, in proportion to its perfection. He early felt and believed that the highest, nay the sole condition of all lasting art is intensity; whence all other necessary conditions must naturally and of themselves proceed. But how difficult, how trying, how exhaustive and all-absorbing, the effort to clothe the intensity of one's feeling with corresponding intensity of expression! Disregarding all considerations of expediency, popularity, profit and personal ease, and in the midst of pecuniary circumstances growing yearly more distressing, Baudelaire still adhered to the single-minded, steadfast artistic purpose, which alone could render possible such artistic effects as his. His art to him, as to every true artist, was more than all the rest of the world. The result, who runs may read. The *Fleurs du Mal*, one small volume, comprises the sum total of Baudelaire's verse. But those few hundreds of lines represent perhaps more sheer force of poetry than Musset and Lamartine rolled into one. Consequently the few hundreds of lines shall live, when many scores of thousands of others shall have passed for ever from the memory of men. Where other poets were content, with so much less trouble and toil, to pour forth a mere dilution, Baudelaire by dint of ceaseless effort and endeavour produced a powerful quintessence, one drop of which will still pervade the mind, whilst a river of the other species of verse may refresh, indeed, and flatter the sense as it flows, but *will* flow, and leave no trace behind. What other latter-day poet, English or French, has such a number of haunting lines? Nothing is more curious to observe than the power of expansion in work of the type of *Les Fleurs du Mal.* With the years, it grows, it quickens instead of fading. "*Les Fleurs du Mal*, livre oublié! Ceci est trop bête. . . On les demande toujours. On commencera peut-être à les comprendre dans quelques années." So wrote Baudelaire, most justly, in response to the remark of some "friend" who had informed him that *Les Fleurs du Mal* were beginning to be forgotten.

Asselineau's account of the covert pride and joy with which Baudelaire, shortly after 1848, showed him the entire MS. of the *Fleurs* beautifully copied out and stitched into a neat binding, is not without its pathos. So much, these verses were to the poet, and so little —then—in the estimation of any one else! The hapless "Flowers" might, indeed, have never appeared in book form at all but for the happy chance of a man of literary taste, Poulet-Malassis, setting up as a publisher and at once bringing out works by Gautier, Banville, Baudelaire and Leconte de Lisle. Needless to say the greatly daring Malassis became eventually a bankrupt. Proper punishment for a man who had actually tried to foist on the public productions of the highest literary art, instead of novels by Alexander Dumas *père*, Octave Feuillet, or Eugène Suë!

Persons who delight in discreditable reports concerning men of letters—whether false or true makes little matter—have read with pleasure in the biography of Baudelaire by M. E. Crépet, published not long since in Paris, that the poet played a not quite admirable part amidst the general agitation of the 1848 revolutionary period. Was it rationally to be expected that a writer, a poet, who for years previously—through the strain of his art no less than owing to the circumstances of his life—had been taxing to the utmost a nervous system naturally delicate and irritable, would upon an occasion of sudden, unforeseen excitement display the soldier-like calm of a Wellington on the field of battle? Had Wellington been placed abruptly in the position of having to write half a dozen pieces of the *Fleurs du Mal* or a series of *Petits Poèmes en Prose*, it is probable that he, too, would have cut a somewhat sorry figure. But, of course, to exact grapes from thorns and figs from oak-trees will, one supposes, remain a favourite amusement of humanity in the future as it always has been in the past.

The years immediately following 1848 saw a somewhat different Baudelaire, physically, from the slender Brummel-like youth with full black locks and half-grown black beard of 1840. Stouter, with hair cropped close, shaven cheeks, and small, somewhat snaky black moustache, the poet, wearing a white blouse and living somewhere in the outskirts of the capital, presented an appearance less poetic though perhaps more revolutionary. Baudelaire's republicanism, however, did not long endure. The Second Empire, to which he was the sooner reconciled by reason of his clear perception of, and extreme contempt for, the democratic fallacy that men in general are units equal and identical in value, aroused in him but little of Victor Hugo's Jovian wrath. He had not, by-the-bye, any of the great poet-politician's personal motives for rage and hatred; no special reason for detesting a *régime*, whose initial crime in M. Hugo's eyes was doubtless its not having set a high enough price upon the suggested if not exactly proffered services of M. Hugo. Only in resentment of the judicial sentence pronounced in 1857 against his *Fleurs du Mal*, might Baudelaire have been stimulated to launch a *Châtiments* of his own. That the six pieces of verse condemned by the Paris Courts were of a nature actually and truly immoral, none knew better than their author. This appears from a passage in his posthumously published diary, where he speaks of "ce livre atroce." The great subject for regret must be that these six pieces were not "condemned" by Baudelaire himself the moment after he had written them. Artistically, as well as morally, they are a blot upon the *ensemble* of the *Fleurs du Mal*. Conceived in a different spirit, they are expressed in a different tone. Bad morality, in the last resort (and in a very different sense from that of the Philistine "moralists," who with characteristic thickness of thought are always confounding the merely unpleasant with the obscene) must be necessarily bad art. In other words, any sentiment base and turbid in itself cannot take on a pure and beautiful artistic expression. All which art touches, art ennobles and refines; that which is not susceptible of being touched by art is of itself ignoble, and remains so.

There is in every man of genius a potential if not actual criminal, as every introspective man of genius well knows. The great thing is not to let the criminal get the upper hand. Baudelaire let loose the criminal too often. Too often he played the part of Hyde to his Dr. Jekyll. And a very lamentable Hyde it is, a dejected and sinister figure, worn and wasted at little more than forty, the shaven haggard face wrinkled, the dark eyes feverishly shining, the neglected locks thin and long and grey, the general attire loose and shabby (shabby, the dandy of early days!) that we behold haunting balls such as that erstwhile odious Casino in the Rue Cadet, and there conversing in cynical callous strain with professional *habituées* of the place; wishing still to produce *effets de surprise* as the man of genius unrecognised, and flying into a fit of "neurasthenic" rage when a "lady" of somewhat more literary turn than the rest confesses acquaintance with but one poet, and that poet—not Baudelaire, but Baudelaire's pet abomination the elegiac Alfred de Musset. Poor Musset! Poor Baudelaire! Poor "lady!" Amazing world!

Baudelaire shortly after 1860 begins to decline. Sainte-Beuve writes to him:—"You have a naturally strong constitution, but your nervous system has been overstrained." Leaving Paris, where his money difficulties threaten to swamp him, he goes to Brussels, expecting to make large sums there by delivering literary lectures. In this attempt he fails, yet does not return to France, but lingers aimlessly on in Belgium, as the stranded vessel settles deeper into the ooze. Without stimulants of some sort, alcohol if opium or haschich be unobtainable, he finds he cannot possibly keep up; solemnly registering meanwhile the most stupendous vows with regard to strict temperance and unflagging labour—in the future. Gradually he becomes incapable of the slightest literary exertion, save that of scribbling in his last hysterical diary, *Mon Cœur mis à nu*, where, amongst other deplorable features, he attacks in terms of the grossest abuse everybody whose views and methods are at all different from his own.

Finally, one afternoon, the doomed man falls helpless on the flags of a Brussels church. Conveyed, a hopeless paralytic, to a hospital near Paris, he there drags out a speechless tragic twelvemouth, so altered that he tries to bow to himself when he catches sight of himself in a mirror, and expires at forty-seven with the mother who adored him literally drinking his last breath as he passes away.

A sad, a dreadful scene to contemplate. A shocking "curtain" to the last act of one of the most painful of life-dramas. Nor can we doubt that Baudelaire ("*j'ai cultivé mon hystérie avec jouissance et terreur*") did much to provoke his fate. But who shall affect to preach sermons over this erring poet's corpse? Who shall come and cast stones of rhetoric upon his tomb? Enough, that he lies there: a man of such gifts, such powers, such aspirations, who came to such an end.

For Charles Baudelaire's epitaph might be proposed his "Harmonie du Soir." For it is full of the white angelic peacefulness we like to think of as hovering over graves.

> "Voici venir les temps où, vibrant sur sa tige,
> Chaque fleur s'évapore ainsi qu'un encensoir;
> Les sons et les parfums tournent dans l'air du soir,
> Valse mélancolique et langoureux vertige.

Chaque fleur s'évapore ainsi qu'un encensoir,
Le violon frémit comme un cœur qu'on afflige,
Valse mélancolique et doulouveux vertige,
Le ciel est triste et beau comme un grand reposoir.

Le violon frémit comme un cœur qu'on afflige,
Un cœur tendre qui haït le néant vaste et noir,
Le ciel est triste et beau comme un grand reposoir,
Le soleil s'est noyé dans son sang qui se fige . . .

Un cœur tendre qui haït le néant vaste et noir
Du passé lumineux receuille tout vestige;
Le soleil s'est noyé dans son sang qui se fige . . .
Ton souvenir en moi luit comme un ostensoir!"

Truly, a lily among the poison-blossoms, a *fleur du bien* among the *Fleurs de Mal*.

CHEZ POUSSET: A LITERARY EVENING.

The eighteenth was a coffee-house century in London as well as Paris. During this nineteenth century the coffee-house has dropped out of London life. But in the French capital it has gone on thriving, and it—or the beerhouse, its equivalent—is still a Parisian institution. Voltaire, Diderot, d'Alembert sat and ruled the empire of letters and, in thought and speech, controlled the spirit of the time, over the cups of *café noir* at the Procope a hundred and twenty or thirty years ago. Men sit now over "*demis*" of Munich brew at Pousset's in the Faubourg Montmartre, and pour forth wit, sarcasm, scorn, poetry, and metaphysics—too often also grossness, meanness, envy, hatred, malice, and all uncharitableness—not unworthy to be the table-talk of Diderot or Voltaire.

The editors of an American magazine once put into execution this idea. They united the cleverest of their contributors at a supposed unceremonious and *entre soi* repast, the while a stenographer sat behind a screen, fixing on his tablets for subsequent publication every flash of *esprit* and fancy, every side-light of experience, knowledge, feeling, emitted under the usual *pendant*- and *après*-dinner influences by the divers gifted guests. The result as it appeared in print was interesting—moderately. It is a pity that such a stenographic "chiel" could not be introduced some night at Pousset's between the hours of twelve and two or three. He might very well be stowed away between the legs of one of those old oak tables in what has been called the *coin des littérateurs*. And then, though somewhat cramped, perhaps, with regard to the disposal of his own legs, presumably longer than the table's, the chiel would be situated admirably for the taking of the oft-quoted notes. More than moderately interesting these would be, as the *littérateurs* who habitually pass the small hours at the *brasserie* near the Place de Châteaudun are neither American nor mediocre.

As one who for years has sat metaphorically at the feet of the Pousset geniuses, and sat literally, though not perhaps always quite comfortably, upon the meagre stamped-leather cushions of the old oak Pousset chairs, let me offer some random reminiscences in default of anything more stenographic.

I.

Midnight, on a balmy spring evening, one of those Paris evenings when the soft air seems filled with a sort of impalpable silver dust. The streets bubbling with people who babble as they go, light-hearted, merry, French. A woman—pretty—strolling carelessly along between two men, looks round her with a little satisfied sigh, and says: "Comme il fait beau ce soir! . . . Il fait bon vivre. . . ."

Flights of the neat little open cabs, with their gleaming fire-fly eyes, are in busy circulation, mostly occupied by couples. From the theatres, the café-chantants, the lounges—from the Champs Elysées and from the Bois de Boulogne—everyone is returning to eat and drink and be merry in the fashionable nocturnal restaurants and cafés.

Three illuminated points in the Rue Royale . . . Weber's, with its customary knot of swells, male and female, in the room to the left, which for long past they have affected, no doubt because it is of too exiguous dimensions to admit more than a picked and chosen few. Larue's, resort of a somewhat cheaper gaiety, on the right-hand corner opposite the Madeleine, the Madeleine showing, on this exquisite May night, so whitely pure and peaceful in the moonlight of Verlaine's verse :—

> " Le calme clair de lune triste et beau,
> Qui fait rêver les oiseaux dans les arbres,
> Et sangloter d'extase les jets d'eau,
> Les grands jets d'eau sveltes parmi les marbres."

And on the other corner, Durand's, which always has been and will be consummately " correct."

To the right-hand, down the boulevards. . . . Hill's, where will be gathered shortly some of the most curiously bad characters of either sex. The Grand Café, not particularly decorous, and yet rather particularly dull. The Café de la Paix, divided into compartments like a train : third class, the room at the back, where persons of the category termed " riff-raff " play at cards with much noise for little money ; second class, the front part, devoted to dominoes and the mildest refreshments ; first-class, the supper-rooms on the Place de l'Opera, overflowing about this hour with a gilded *jeunesse.* To pursue this metaphor, the private rooms upstairs, where people of a smarter description sometimes find themselves when they wish to vary their venue from Bignon's or the Maison d'Or, might be likened to Pullman cars. Altogether "la Paix" is not dissimilar from a rambling ramshackle train, making night hideous with its clatter and crowded to excess, as it pants its way along rails of vice and folly, with travellers paying far too much for their tickets.

Further on, other cafés. . . . Cabs and *coupés* by the hundred line the sidewalk in front of them, and crowds of orderly "consumers" sit at the little round-topped tables on the "terrace." Julien's, of the big and blazing order, highly "modern" in the worst sense: debauchery at wholesale prices, a sort of "stores" for the dispensing of adulterated drinkables, eatables such as had best be left uneaten, and—the rest. Immediately alongside of Julien's (in obedience perhaps to the law of contrasts) the old established "Napolitain," one of the best of Paris cafés, where the company is generally on a par with the ices and liqueurs. And close by the Vaudeville Theatre, opposite, the Café Américain, vilest perhaps of all, whose name embodies a satire upon a nation which, with all its faults and shortcomings, has done nothing to deserve such treatment at the hands of a sister Republic.

Several hundreds of yards before the next batch of boulevard cafés is reached. Why, in

Paris, should cafés thus hang together? One might imagine they fear solitude, and yearn to be ever in each other's company, when one sees how, from one end of the boulevards to the other, extensive café-less patches are succeeded by spots where two or three or more of the places are huddled one on top of the other. Here, on the Boulevard des Italiens, is a sort of spurious Pousset's; a branch, an offshoot, not *the* Pousset's, only an exoteric *succursale* of the establishment whose esoteric centre is in the Faubourg Montmartre. To this latter haunt it is now high time to repair. The other cafés along the boulevards—Zimmer's, the Café de Suède, Café Garen, Café des Princes—are worth neither a visit nor a mention.

II.

From twelve to half-past, a good time to arrive at Pousset's. Vacant seats are few, but celebrities many. Inside and outside, the place is packed. And when we reflect that to each of these "consumers," who has his place taken by another consumer the very instant he departs, corresponds at least one and generally more than one big mug of Munich beer, we are not surprised at the fact that a special train runs daily from the Bavarian capital to Paris, freighted solely with the produce of Löwenbraü, Spatenbraü, and other Braüs claiming doubtless to be equally first-rate. A great German victory, greater than Worth or Sedan. French patriots may, and do, declaim and rave. The only answer to their objurgations is, that if German beer is not to be drunk in France, then France must fabricate beer of her own at least as good if not better.

On making good one's entrance into the famous *brasserie* of the wits, one pauses and looks around with some bewilderment. Such crowding, such clattering of glasses and plates, such Babel noise of tongues, such apparent general confusion; such rushing of white-aproned waiters to and fro, bearing aloft foaming tankards of the topaz-hued liquid all a-glitter under the bluish glare of electric light! The decoration of the room, with its dark tones of old oak and Spanish leather, dim faded hues of tapestry hangings, freshness of faiences here and there on the walls and richness of handsome stained-glass windows, is, in its elaborately designed effect of mediævalism, harmonious and pleasing to the eye. But attendants and customers too are as un-mediæval as could possibly be imagined. At first sight, a motley crew; a company about as composite as in the street outside.

The situation of Pousset's, for a place which from the first has had its aspects of *chic*-ness, is un-*chic* to a degree. The Faubourg Montmartre, by night especially, is one of the nastiest thoroughfares in Paris. The Strand, only worse; if worse than the Strand during hours of darkness be conceivable to the mind of man. That Place de Châteaudun, too, at the corner of which Pousset's stands, is not improper only, but *bourgeois* in its commonplaceness of impropriety. Yet people for years past have patronised Pousset's who perhaps would hesitate to honour it with their presence were it situated in any better part of the town.

Notwithstanding Pousset's fashionable and literary vogue, persons neither fashionable nor literary nor anything else that is mentionable to ears polite will often force in their way from out their native gutter. But they soon find it is not their element. Visibly they don't enjoy having to be on their good behaviour, and are generally inclined to vote Pousset's (as I once heard said by a gentleman of essentially Faubourg-Montmartrean appearance who was being turned ruthlessly and bodily away from the temple of old oak and stained glass) a " sale boîte," fit only for "des sales aristos." Pousset's is not sufficiently democratic for the denizens of the "Faubourg du Crime."

Fashion at Pousset's—that is represented by, here and there, seated in the more comfortable corners, a certain number of men and women (men *with* women *cela va sans dire*) whose smartness is genuine enough. To-night there has been a *première* at one of the best theatres. So Pousset is attracting not only several of the critics, but also a batch of first-nighters, who stand or sit and look about them as if they were come to seek a sixth act to the performance. Quite a theatrical evening, indeed, at this pothouse. Appropriately accompanied, here are several well-known ladies of the boards. Ensconced at one of the tables near the door, that woman with the small pretty features, melting eye, and delicate porcelain complexion. . . She is charmingly dressed in white and Nile-green silk, with a bonnet of the kind that any lady would immediately and truthfully pronounce "a love." It is an actress of the Français with her good and respected mother—a mother of the monumental type which actresses, the world over, would seem to revel in. That other attractive face, straight proud little nose, delicate Cupid's bow mouth, brow fresh and smooth beneath the *bandeaux à la vierge*—another actress, of the Gymnase, or is it the Vaudeville now? . . . I forget. Here again, an interesting female visage, sharp expression, keen eye, and rather Gavroche air generally. It isn't her expression only that is sharp. *Pour plus amples détails*, enquire of the lady's lady friends.

Histrions of the other sex also are here to-night, more numerous, if less delightful. Those two little shrivelled old men, sitting huddled up together, as like as two twins. . . . Twins they are; *ils s'y sont mis à deux*, as Scholl said, *pour nous embêter davantage*. Anxious roving black eyes, wizened smooth-shaven visages, long locks thrown back with that displeasing careful carelessness, sure mark of a nature filled with vulgar conceit; for forty years past they have been singing, reciting, attending at all funerals of eminent artists, and otherwise thrusting their little joint individuality upon a public which has long since tired of the same. And now they are stranded, high and dry, upon two stamped leather seats at the *brasserie* Pousset, with none "so kind to do them" a *demi* or even a *quart* of Munich beer. Not long ago they brought out a volume of *Souvenirs*. Amusing, but not exactly in the places where amusement was meant. "Reminiscences" of that kind are what readers generally prefer to forget.

A heavily-lined close-shaven face, with grey hair showing beneath the brim of an extraordinary hat. . . . Plays he has written, theatres he has directed; or rather these latter have directed him, towards the Bankruptcy Court, if current report is to be believed. Was it he, or some other fellow-creature bearing his by no means unusual patronymic, who perpetrated that most pathetic apostrophe in a five-act drama in verse to "cette *table* qui t'a vu naître?"

. . . A pretty boy with another pretty boy. Both nicely clothed, scarfed, and hatted (a thing rare enough in Paris to be made a note of when found) and both completely conscious of these facts. Pretty boy No. 1's full smooth face with the peculiar bright-eyed expression recalls instantly to mind his clever sister, now dead, who held at the Francais a more prominent position than he, one fears, will ever do. But one imagines that life, for him, contains other successes than those to be won at the Comédie Française. Pretty boy No. 2: recent *prix de comédie* at the Conservatoire, looked on by himself and by admiring friends, of the feminine gender more especially, as a Delaunay of the future.

A face bearing every mark of intelligence and sympathetic power; it belongs to the young and brilliantly successful manager of the Théâtre Libre. The face of his companion, one of the cracks of the Théâtre Libre troupe: coarse and rather sneering just at present (the pair are doubtless talking about a friend) but not without a certain look of force. Enter a gentleman fresh from England. He promptly sits himself down to *écrevisses* along with a *demi* of beer and relates a tale of a London manager which the French manager considers amusing. Perhaps there are anecdotes about the French manager that might be considered amusing by the English one.

Playwrights, like poets, are an irritable genus, and several of them are venting their irritation here to-night. That young one—so young, but already so fat!—is the author of a farce which, when first produced, was hailed by Sarcey with Comanche yells of delight. "Ce petit . . . ," Sarcey wrote (though why "petit," seeing the gentleman is very nearly as large around the waist as M. Sarcey himself?) "ce petit . . . ira loin." *Ce petit* has not since betrayed any particular anxiety to realise the prediction. He may "go far" yet, but, if so, he will have to do it pretty quickly. Along with him is a man much bigger than he: speaking not literally but figuratively.

His face at once reminds you of his plays. Massive and full; a firm clear glance, from under well-marked brows; a mouth, soft and sensitive yet not exactly weak, under a stiffly-clipped moustache. But the chin, that pasty chin, in which the strength of all the rest of the countenance is belied! His chin it is which gives him away. *Desinit in piscem* applies to both the visage and the pieces. They begin, these pieces, most effectively and powerfully; progress happily, then fall away to nothing towards the close. Genius, perhaps, but he can't keep it up for more than two acts out of five. This must be trying to the temper; and explains, no doubt, his being so querulous and complaining. At this very moment he is saying, in his raspingest voice, vinegary things to his companion, who listens with one ear and, with one eye, glances indifferent assent. "—— est arrivé en se plaignant," somebody said lately. "He has complained his way into success." Smart enough, if you like, but on the whole quite untrue. Where we should be, though, and how continue to exist, if we were not always saying untruths about each other, is impossible to imagine.

III.

Not fashionables, not actresses and actors, not dramatists, not even *écrevisses* and beer, are the chief attraction *chez Pousset.* These things are either not worth having, or may be had in equal perfection elsewhere. What one has really come for is the presence and conversation of the geniuses.

They are distinguishable easily among even the large crowd here assembled. Unmistakable, at all times and in all places, is the stamp of superior intellect, that sets apart those marked with it from the ordinary un-idead herd, like the shepherd's dog as contrasted with his flock.

Almost every night that score of men come to take up that little quarter of their own in the corner, where half-a-dozen tables are set end to end against the tapestried wall. They split themselves usually into groups forming part of a whole, as do the nebulæ in the Milky Way; and then to the accompaniment *obbligato* of beer and smoke, and ham and sourcrout and crayfish (to such Germanic uses are Parisian palates now put), they, night after night, hour after hour, up to two or three A.M., sit realising Lee's line on Alexander, slightly altered:—

> "Then *they* will talk—ye gods! how *they* will talk!"

Most admirable and otherwise remarkable among the talkers is the fashionable poet and *conteur*, whom his friends call fondly and familiarly "Catulle." A face filled with the finest kind of beauty, of hue, of feature, of expression. Long soft light hair, thinning but slightly—at fifty years of age!—over the crown of the head, and untouched with the least thread of grey. Smooth brow; large eyes veiled by drooping lids; a nose of noble shape, its Hebraism apparent only in a slight peculiarity of the nostril's curve. The rounded gentle contour of cheek and chin is framed by a beard graceful as the frondage of the fern. His countenance recalls that of Fra Angelico's Christ; yet, somehow, in spite (or because) of its smoothness, softness, suavity, it is suggestive, rather horribly, of that corruption which is the soul of his art.

As art, however, this art is superb. The faculty of distinguishing and appropriating the special note of beauty in the work of other men, is in him developed to excess. "Il fait," as some one once said of him, "du bon n'mporte qui." *Du bon* Gautier, *du bon* Hugo, *du bon* Leconte de Lisle, *du bon* Verlaine. *Du bon* anybody and everybody, both in prose and verse. Those scrofulous little stories of his are, no less than his poems, in point of execution quite masterly and unique; and altogether, with his extraordinary passion for beauty, and utter natural obliviousness to what the modern world calls moral sense, he seems a figure from the days of classical decay.

To hear him speak reminds one of that old saying of the "golden mouth." The grace, facility, fluency, freedom of his utterance and expression are delightful. He wreathes words together, by the hundred, as one might wreathe the loveliest flowers. Around and about every subject that they touch his periods entwine themselves like creepers in adornment. At this moment he is expatiating on Théodore de Banville, and dwelling, with wealth of term, upon that poet's peculiar "exteriority." "Banville is exactly what a fruit would be if it were all smooth satin rind, with nothing at all beneath." Villiers de l'Isle Adam achieved something still better in this direction, when he defined Henry Fouquier, the *chroniqueur*, as a Zero. "And not even the line which circumscribes the Zero. But the empty space circumscribed, the inner nothingness, the interior blank and void."

Of Villiers, it may truly be said that he was faithful to Pousset's unto death. A few days before succumbing to a variety of ills, among which pennilessness was probably the worst, he came as usual to the *brasserie* and drank three *quarts* (that is a French word, not an English) merely because he hadn't enough in his pocket to pay for two *demis.* Villiers was the author of some tales highly admirable in their way, and of verses among which these, through the sheer force of expressiveness, remain present to my mind—

> "Ses crimes évoqués sont tels qu'on croit entendre
> *La crosse des fusils sonner sur le palier.*"

The poet here is not referring to his friend Catulle, as some uncharitable persons might pretend to suppose, but to some imaginary female with whom Villiers is in love. Her iniquity morbidly attracts him, as the unspeakable idiocy of the "catoplébas," that animal so stupid that it ate off its own feet, attracted the hermit in Flaubert's *Tentation de Saint Antoine.* Villiers' powers as a conversationalist were enormous. His knowledge seemed surpassingly various and vast, for his memory was like the tablets of the Recording Angel, from which no line, no letter, once inscribed, can ever thenceforth be effaced. To request Villiers to recall some verse or couplet out of, for example, *Poèmes Barbares* or *La Légende des Siècles*, was hardly prudent: he would immediately proceed to recite the whole. In his vague quavering monotone, he would render the light and shade of an entire piece, his effects of elocution somehow making one think of those great, grey, melancholy frescoes by Puvis de Chavannes, that seem to live with a dream-life of their own. Whether Villiers was actually crazy, is not easy to decide. If he were, it is perhaps a matter for regret that so many other people should be sane.

. . . A bald pate, pug-nose, small, twinkling black eyes, and rough, rather long black beard: decidedly this other gentleman looks so like the great Greek sage, Plato's tutor, as for a moment to set one thinking of the doctrine of metempsychosis. His literary genius lies in his strange originalty of thought, combined with his terseness, freshness, vigour of expression. The most difficult of Hugo's rhythms he swings with the dexterousness of a David twirling his sling. And Stupidity is the great Goliath, which his verse hits full in the forehead every time:—

> "Car je le dis et le répète
> *On n'est pas bon quand on est bête.*"

That is satire, because it is truth.

It was to him that Verlaine addressed his little pot-house ode:—

"Bois pour oublier!
L'eau de vie est une
Qui porte la lune
Dans son tablier. . . .

. . . .

L'injure des hommes
Qu'est-ce que ça fait?
Va, notre cœur sait
Seul ce que nous sommes."

"*Drink* in order to *forget*" . . . One cannot tell whether Ponchon has succeeded in attaining the latter desideratum, but judging from the quantity of little round pieces of felt on the table before him, each separately representing a *demi* already absorbed, with more *demis* still coming, one perceives he is at least persistently putting into practice the former part of his friend's poetic advice.

Verlaine himself now sits beside him. Bald, like Ponchon, and similarly not to be congratulated on his beard. Rough-hewn expressive nose; ardent eyes, set slightly sideways in the head like a faun's; eager, sensitive, contorted mouth. He seems sad. I have never seen him otherwise, unless indeed he was either scornful or enraged. He raises to his seamed and wrinkled brow a withered and slightly trembling hand, and stolidly stares awhile at the big glass of beer before him.

Note, not far off, that Lucius Verus head, with its curled fleecy shock, black, but besprinkled here and there with snow. Bold features, yet a certain delicacy and fineness about the profile. Since his Sarah Bernhardt days, this famous French poet, *nouvelliste*, novelist and playwright, has married and settled down and appears but rarely at the *brasseries* he used so assiduously to frequent. If he is here to-night at Pousset's it is doubtless for no other reason than to be sketched. There is a rather puffed-up look about his face. His verses are sometimes rather puffed-up too. He prides himself on immense, almost brutal power. But at bottom he is sentimental, kind, and perhaps a little weak. He has written one admirable book, the story of an ardent, erring young poet, graceful, delicate, frail, and gentle as a woman, yet full of spirit and pride. I have often thought that herein this pseudo-truculent literary "blasphemer" hadn't far to look for his model.

And now this other poet, with the graceful smile and somewhat debased expression of the eye. A poet who devotes nearly the whole of his time and talent to the concoction, for high pay, of bestial stories in the worst of the Boulevard prints. With him, a wit of the spasmodic order, whose sole end and object in existence is to make the *Gil Blas's* readers smile and the diners at club tables roar. Again, a young *chroniqueur* distinguished for peculiar astringency of *esprit*, yet afflicted with a sincere lyric taste—he quoted to me once in the streets at three o'clock in the morning the whole of Victor Hugo's *Abeilles*, with a feeling which "l'aïeul" himself would have approved. His companion is another journalist, the type of the irresistible seducer. All is fish that comes within the net of his delightful, da Vincian smile. Not effeminate, not exactly feminine even, but one of those men who appear to have stolen from women whatever is subtlest and finest in their femininity, for the sole purpose and with the sole design of penetrating more quickly and surely to the centre of their nature. He was born with, and he exerts constantly to the full, the great Cleopatra instinct of charming all, always, among the opposite sex. I can see him as I sat with him one Sunday going to Asnières by train, a yellow rose in the button-hole of his grey frock coat. On the seat in front of us was a girl, timid, only slightly pretty, and obviously respectable, although alone. Some governess perhaps, or some *première* in a nice Rue de la Paix kind of shop. My companion, who knew naturally, that just then he was looking his best—and his best is no uninteresting or unattractive thing—bent forward slightly with his air of being so ready to adore, and mutely offered her his flower. She, poor child! blushed suddenly to the whites of her eyes, sat holding the yellow rose in the palm of her little hand, and on arriving at her destination (which was different from ours) in her confusion got out on the wrong side. Poor girl! who knows how long and how much she may have dwelt since then upon that incident in the Asnières train?

Other figures in Pousset's literary corner: a melancholy-looking young man of partly English parentage, with a sincere and delicate talent too slight to force great public recognition; a long-haired poet of the sensuo-mystico-symbolic school, much more "sensual" in appearance than he is either of the other things; his companion, a minor "realist," small, vivid, gracious face, Dresden China-like in its delicacy of complexion; two well-known *chroniqueurs* of the *fin de siècle* school, one with a singularly acute expression of countenance, quite the air of being somebody, and yet so narrowly escaping the being nobody after all; the other, bold, virile and contemptuous in glance and port, the strongest "temperament" among all the younger novelists and free-lances of the press; last of all, a towering pot-house æsthete, next door to nothing as to actual results, but as to potentiality, a giant; an ever-seething volcano of science, lyrism, satire, passion, poison, and in one word—which must be a French word, English possessing no equivalent—a *raté titanesque.*

"Le Café des Ratés," indeed, is what an English friend of mine suggested that Pousset's should be entitled. But this would hardly be correct, for the real *ratés* among the geniuses at Pousset's are but few. The majority of them are doing their own work in their own way, which, must mean, if anything does, fruition. True, these are the least powerful and least gifted of the lot; in accordance, no doubt, with the fatal law that the stronger the genius the less the chances of its coming freely and fully to light. But what then? Is not genius, in the main, self-sufficing; a kingdom unto itself, a world, a Heaven, and also, alas, a Hell?

. . . Va, notre cœur sait
Seul ce que nous sommes!"

Paul Verlaine's view, the right one.

IV.

The sitting perforce is drawing to a close. Final despairing cries for *demis* or even for *quarts*, for *fines*, for whiskeys (pronounced here "veeskee"), and especially for *kümmel*, are unavailing to attract the notice of harassed *garçons* intent on claiming the settlement of the evening's accounts. "Messieurs, trois heurs; on ferme!" shouts a "gérant," the size of his voice in inverse ratio to that of his frame. But still the talk goes on at the literary tables, more fragmentary, more spasmodic now, but perhaps also more brilliant; like gold-bearing rock broken up very small; the more minute the pieces, the more they shine.

* * * *

"Ohé, l'homme aux vers de dix-neuf pieds et demi! Prête-m'en deux, je ne plus me servir des miens."

* * * *

"Une chronique, dix chroniques, mille chroniques, et jamais un mot! Est-ce qu'on a le droit d'écrire sans jamais faire des mots? Jésus-Christ lui-même a fait des mots . . . . C'est pour ça qu'on en parle encore."

* * * *

"Balzac—un grand poète né sans voix . . . . Une lyre énorme sans cordes."

* * * *

"Un tel? C'est une canaille . . . Je le connais, je suis comme lui."

"Il est pourri, c'est vrai . . . Mais ce qu'il fait est d'un art! . . . Que voulez-vous . . . Il faut du fumier à la racine des fleurs."

* * * *

"Allons, allons, dépêchons-nous, on ferme! Ca va finir mal—comme une pièce de Becque."

"Becque? ne vous gênez pas pour lui . . . Il est parti depuis une heure."

"Eh bien, suivons son exemple."

And now the symposium breaks up. Outside, the cool greyness of the morning streets, with, just perceptible in the fleecy sky, the first warm suggestion of a brilliant day. Cabs, of a kind, are still to be had near by. So some of the literary revellers are driven to baccarat at the clubs, others to supper at the Americain upstairs, others again – a prudent few – home to their bed.

GUY DE MAUPASSANT.

I.

The old book-keeper, M. Leras, who for forty years has sat day after day in the self-same office on the same high chair, comes out one afternoon and is tempted to a solitary stroll. He doesn't particularly feel the hardship of his fate. "Having never enjoyed anything, he had no particular desires." On this occasion he is even rather cheerful; he actually treats himself to a little dinner with a half-bottle of cheap Bordeaux at a corner wine-shop, where he sits at a square tin table, painted yellow, without any cloth on it, outside on the pavement near the establishment's wide-open door. Then he has a cup of black coffee and a glass of *fine champagne*, and by way of making an evening of it, wanders off in the direction of the Bois de Boulogne. Darkness gradually gathers. The summer air is breathless. All along the broad white avenue that leads into the great fashionable park, rolls an interminable string of open cabs with their fire-fly eyes, each cab containing, invariably a couple. A subtle fever of desire and passion stirs abroad like a whispering breeze. Leras reflects; desire—love—passion—little enough has *he* ever had to do with that! . . . Night falls, and fatigued, he sits down upon a bench. And now forms of prowling women come about him: prostitution, in its lowest, most abominable guise, the prostitution of utter penury, of snatching eagerness for the smallest sum; prostitution that disgraces the scenes where in darkness it ventures to lurk, as an open sewer would disgrace a splendid street: its contact, its mere aspect, bring sadness upon his heart. This, then, he thinks, is life: pleasure, wealth, gaity, dissipation in rolling carriages, unheard-of depths of degradation amid the gloom, and for some—as for him—life-long solitude in jail-like offices and bare, sinister garret rooms. His room . . . it seems impossible for him to go back to it. . . . A nameless wretchedness, an inevitable grief, a sense of awful despair possess him. . . . As though to get away from something, he rises and hastens off—deep off—into the wooded alleys of the park beyond its iron gate. Finally he turns into a thicket, and there, next morning early, is found the body of an old man who has hanged himself with his braces. It is the sort of periodical occurrence to which the newspapers devote a par. Guy de Maupassant has made of it a thing tragic enough for Dante.

Monsieur Parent, a kindly, slow, timid man with a wife who despises and deceives him. All the love in his nature, which can find no other vent, is centred on the baby son. At length a family cataclysm. The woman, with perversion's fiendish instinct for striking straight at the most vulnerable part, spits out at him, among a flood of other taunts, the fact that the boy is not his. And then, taking the child, she goes to live with Monsieur Parent's former friend, her lover. The wronged and wretched man is left alone. Years pass. He sinks into a kind of torpor. Each day on the same bench in the same café for hours; when thinking least, he is least unhappy. And thus he grows gradually old. One summer's day, friends prevail upon him to go and spend the afternoon at Saint-Germain. He has dinner there at the Pavillon Henri Quatre, and from a distance recognises the trio who all these years have been living upon an allowance from him. Wife, lover, boy, the boy now grown into a tall, conceited-looking young man. Parent's blood boils: his wasted, miserable life—these are the wretches that have wrecked it! But he will be revenged on them—on all three. How? he feverishly considers, as he sits and more narrowly examines them. The woman—she is stout now, and looks contemptuous; she seems precisely the sort of person who would be hardest on any failing or weakness in others. The man—well-preserved, well-dressed, air of diplomatic dignity; he, Parent, is shambling, almost shabby, heavy, weak, bald, and prematurely grey. Oh, but he will tell them what he thinks of them—tell them boldly what they are . . . Their copious, carefully chosen meal well over, the three walk off into the wood. The young man, full of spirits, leaps like a colt over the fallen trees. But now Monsieur Parent is upon them. The repressed pain and resentment of twenty years pour from his lips in a long, heated, incoherent, undignified tirade. The others stand and stare at him without a word, until at last he ambles angrily and excitedly away. That night at his Paris café he drinks, for the first time in his life, more than is good for him, and is sent home by the *patron* in a cab. Not romantic—but *c'est la vie.*

Jean de Servigny, typically Parisian, slight, elegant, apparently frail but in reality indefatigable, light, sceptical, changeable, at once irresolute and energetic, capable of everything and of nothing, finds himself attracted to the daughter of the "Marquise Obardi"—*marquise pour rire.* Yvette, young, intelligent, charming, has been brought up in luxury to believe her mother a real *grande dame.* But slowly things have dawned upon her, and when she "finds out" for certain she wants to die; to die in a carefully-prepared, slightly theatrical manner, for in the midst of her native goodness and *naïveté* and delicacy, she still, by inherited tendency, is histrionic. So after a day at her mother's place on the river when more than ever she has made herself fascinating in the eyes of the whole male party assembled, she inhales chloroform from a lot of little bottles that, with much pains, she has procured from as many different chemists. Die, however, she doesn't, for an alarm is given and Jean de Servigny breaks into her room. She cares for Servigny, and now she lets him know it. He is deeply moved and touched, but under the circumstances what is a man to do? Poor Yvette! for all her girlish dreams, she will tread in the "marchioness's" footsteps. *C'est la vie.*

The old husband, whose wife has dragged him to a town on the Norman coast, rebels when she speaks of going out walking in the fields on one of the hottest days of the whole summer, and turns her over to M. d'Apreval, their joint friend and companion for many years. The first words between the pair when they start reveal that they are bent on a painful errand. They are going, by Madame de Cadour's wish, into the interior to catch sight of a man who lives there, pensioned, ignorant of his origin, and in reality is their illegitimate son. And all along the way, along the hot, white, dusty road beneath the blinding glare of the sun, Madame de Cadour ponders painfully over the past. She had been married, as in France so many girls are married, to a man who was virtually a stranger. A friend, M. d'Apreval, had long loved her with profound, persistent passion; her husband one day left for a distant voyage, and resistance was possible no further. A child was born of their love, and now Madame de Cadour, for the first time since his birth when she was obliged to send him away, is going to feast her eyes upon her son. . . The pair arrive at the farm the son has bought with his unknown mother's supplies. She sees him, and her heart sinks into the ground. A coarse, rude peasant, married to a woman ruder, coarser still. The old lady and the old gentleman pretend they have come in merely to get a glass of milk; the two peasants eye them suspiciously and churlishly, and Madame de Cadour and M. d'Apreval depart. Slowly they retrace their way—he mute, she shedding incessant tears—along the same white, straight, interminable road. On their reaching home the husband, who has enjoyed meanwhile a comfortable nap, asks them if they have had "une jolie promenade." "Charmante, mon cher, tout à fait charmante," is M. d'Apreval's reply.

Hautot *père*, the middle-aged, well-to-do Norman farmer, half-gentleman, half-peasant, is proud of his land and fond of his shooting. With a party of his friends, he goes out for partridge one morning early. He brings one down, and runs into the brushwood to get it. The next moment a report is heard. "Ha! ha!" the friends exclaim, "he must have lighted on a hare!" But Hautot doesn't re-appear. They go to look for him, and find him lying helpless with the contents of his second barrel in his body. Hautot *fils*, a tall, lank, somewhat simple and timid young man, stands the next day by his father's bedside watching him pass away. Such an accident—so sudden—he can hardly realise the situation. But Hautot *père* can realise it, and is prepared. One last injunction he has to make, too delicate for writing, or for any ears save those of his son. A widower for many years past, farmer Hautot has had a female friend. His death will make a terrible difference in her position, and out of a sentiment of honour, he wishes his son to visit her and assure her she will not be left to want. Hautot *fils* promises; the father dies and is buried, and the next week sees the son ringing at the door of an apartment on the third floor of an old house in the large town near by. A pretty, pleasing, fresh-faced, modest woman ("aimante, dévouée, une vraie femme, quoi," the father had said of her on his death-bed) receives him, and is overwhelmed at the news he imparts. M. Hautot dead! this very day she had been expecting him. At the table in the dining-room his place is ready laid; almost impossible to realise that he will never sit there any more! But "Mam'zelle Donet" reflects that Hautot *fils* may be hungry after his journey. She presses him to eat; reluctantly, timidly, he consents, and the pair sit down together with a little boy who at first, on seeing his mother weep, had fallen frantically upon the unknown visitor and kicked and beaten his ankles and thighs. Mam'zelle Donet declines to accept the yearly sum Hautot *fils* has been directed by the dead man to offer. She can make her own living, as she always has done before. But at length, "If I do accept," she murmurs, "it shall be settled on the little one." On the little one! César Hautot understands. And long and wistfully he looks at the unconscious little fellow now busy with fork and knife. —When the young man at last rises clumsily to go, Mam'zelle Donet is at a loss what to say to him. Hautot *père* was in the habit of coming once a week to have early dinner with Mam'zelle Donet and Master Emile. . . Hautot *fils*, still much upset and bewildered, is invited to return the week following, and he accepts.

Boitelle is an old peasant who goes from farm to farm performing the vilest kind of drudgery for a pittance. He is married, and has fourteen children, all alive, and, as peasants go, doing well. Why, then, should he have fallen so low? Because, he explains, his parents wouldn't let him marry as he wished. When young and a soldier he had a strange fondness for exotic things. He would stand by the hour in the streets of Hâvre, lost in admiration at the sight of the lately-landed tropical birds with their strange, rich, variegated plumage. One day he meets a young negress with eyes like jet beads, and glistening teeth, and headdress of sumptuous yellow and red, and she appears to him a creature glorious and gorgeous as the birds. He falls in love, and at length proposes, and one day takes her into the country to see his parents and get their consent. She does her best to ingratiate them; turns up her sleeves to help the mother in kitchen and farmyard, and is attentive and cheerful and respectful. But alas, a blackamoor! "Non, vrai, all' est *trop* noire," the bewildered parents murmur, in response to their son's entreaties. With heavy heart he takes his negress back in all her finery to the station, whilst troops of country folk come flocking to view the spectacle of a weeping black woman arm-in-arm with "le fi' Boitelle." A French peasant's reverence for the paternal will causes Boitelle to relinquish his dream of exotic passion. But his life is never the same again. His subsequent marriage and the fourteen children themselves bring him no joy. Careless of everything, he gradually sinks. He had once a glimpse of what would have been happiness to him but didn't obtain it. . . That is all.

Finally, the fierce, disdainful, dandified, feline little German officer who, during an orgy in the *château* which "Mlle. Fifi" and his brother officers are occupying in Normandy towards the close of the Franco-German campaign, blows smoke from his big porcelain pipe into the mouth of his temporary female companion, and follows up the compliment by heaping opprobrium upon the defeated French. The woman snatches a knife off the table, stabs him to death, and escapes into the darkness without. By the care of the village priest, she is hidden in the belfry, and the raging German officers beat the country for a month and never find her. After the war she is married by a citizen, "sans préjugés," who makes of her, in Guy de Maupassant's semi-sardonic, semi-patriotic phrase, "une Dame qui valut autant que beaucoup d'autres."

II.

The six or seven tales I have sought to summarise above—*Promenade*, *Monsieur Parent*, *Yvette*, *L'Abandonné*, *Hautot Père et Fils*, *Boitelle* and *Mlle. Fifi*—are among Guy de Maupassant's gems. Many others of his are no less perfect. *Miss Harriett*, for example, is a favourite with French readers, if to a foreign taste not quite so satisfying. The figure of the sentimental English spinster, who distributes tracts broadcast to the peasants of the Norman coast, and, having fallen in love with an irresistible French painter, throws herself into a well because she sees him kiss the maid-servant, though intended perhaps to be touching, is a little farcical in reality. *Madame Baptiste* is tragic, terrible, harrowing, to a point which renders it unsuitable for a short description. *Deux Amis*, the two timorous, inoffensive *bourgeois*, who towards the end of the Paris siege, venture beyond the fortifications to the riverside to fish, where they are caught by the

Prussians and incontinently shot for spies: this is life, life itself, in its inadequacy of cause and horror of result. Again, the little story entitled *Adieu:* how well it renders the infinite sadness of age, that creeps so quickly over human beings, turning the gay gallant into a decrepit old man, and the delicate, exquisite girl into a red-faced stout matron! Crime long hidden rising irresistibly to the criminal's lips beside a deathbed, is an old theme, treated however with new force in *La Confession. La Petite Roque* is quite fearful in its indication of involuntary and almost unconscious bestiality and crime. The everyday tragedy of suppressed affection is touched with singular tenderness in *Mademoiselle Perle. Le Père Amable* is surprising for the sharpness with which it throws into relief the harsher qualities of the Norman peasant's nature.

In *L'Inutile Beauté*, there is something imposing about the directness with which the physiological discrepancies of humanity are brought into question. *Le Champ d'Oliviers* is high tragedy. The little riverside narrative, *Mouche*, is at once pathetic and droll. *L'Héritage* is "horrible, most horrible" in its delineation of *bourgeois* meanness and baseness. Especially admirable is *Garçon, un bock!* which in half a dozen pages shows the disintegration of an over-sensitive nature through the effects of a premature vision of the hidden horrors of life. "C'était une âme très-délicate, tres-fine, originale et tendre, qui s'est fêlée au premier choc de là vie." That applies to the hero of *Garçon, un bock!* no less than it did to Charles Baudelaire, of whom it was originally said. Excellent, again, is the story called *Mon Oncle Jules*, relating the experience of the little boy who has always heard his people brag about an absent uncle who will one day return to shed distinction upon them all. This relative finally turns up in the person of a broken-down wretch who opens oysters on a steamboat for his living. Only the boy discovers who it is, but he already knows enough of the world in general and his progenitors in particular to keep his counsel under circumstances like these. He sees no more of his vagrant uncle. But often afterwards he thinks of him, and gives abundant alms to the poor.

One sees that Guy de Maupassant at his best is consistently melancholy and dark. His other vein of quaint Norman humour, appears all the brighter by comparison. *Toine*, for instance, is astonishingly (though rather coarsely) comic. "Ah oui, on le connaissait. Toine Brûlot, le plus gros homme du canton, et même de l'arrondissement.

Sa petite maison semblait dérisoirement trop étroite et trop basse pour le contenir, et quand on le voyait debout sur sa porte ou il passait des journées entières, on se demandait comment il pourrait entrer dans sa demeure. Il y rentrait chaque fois que se présentait un consommateur, car Toine-ma-Fine était invité de droit à prélever son petit verre sur tout ce qu'on buvait chez lui." This Falstaffian Norman innkeeper has a wife, as thin and shrewish as he is fat and gay—"elle était née de mauvaise humeur et elle avait continué à être mécontente de tout." She is for ever abusing him; he in reply merely chortles, so long as he keeps well and strong. But when he gets paralysed and is bed-ridden, Madame Toine has her innings, and well she plays it. She refuses flatly to give him any food, unless he will hatch out as many of her chickens' eggs for her as she can manage to insinuate between his arms and body. Dreadfully humiliated, he is obliged to consent. Playing dominoes with his still faithful cronies under circumstances such as these is indeed an affliction and a trial, and when at last the truth becomes known to old Toine's bedside companions their merriment and mockery knows no bounds. He one day breaks several of the eggs by making an imprudent movement, whereupon his wife comes in and beats him violently before the others. "Les trois amis de Toine riaient à suffoquer, toussant, éternuant, poussant des cris, et le gros homme effaré parait les attaques de sa femme *avec prudence, pour ne point casser encore les cinq œufs qu'il avait de l'autre côté.*" Finally, despite all difficulties and doubts, every single chicken is successively and successfully brought to the light of day, and when the last one breaks its shell, "Toine, affolé de joie, délivré, glorieux, baisa sur le dos le frêle animal faillit l'étouffer avec ses levres. Il voulut le garder dans son lit, celui-là, jusqu' au lendemain, saisi par une tendresse de mère pour cet être si fretiot qu' il avait donné à la vie ; mais la vieille l'emporta comme les autres sans écouter les supplications de son homme."

Le Rosier de Madame Husson, Tribunaux Rustiques, La Ficelle, La Bête à Maît' Belhomme, and many more, are in this same vein of robust and simple drollery, And indeed, when M. Lemaître, as literary critic of the *Revue Bleue* of Paris, first treated of Guy de Maupassant some eight or ten years ago, he chose to regard this powerful pessimistic spirit as merely a master of peasant comicality, a sort of Norman *Molière de Village*. M. Lemaître, however, has since made the *amende honorable*. He had, it seems, met M. de Maupassant, and finding him "bien portant, un peu haut en couleur," with "l'air d'un robuste bourgeois campagnard," had concluded that art, and the author of *Toine* and *Tribunaux Rustiques* would never have much in common. And yet there is a proverb in M. Lemaître's language which says, "Il ne faut pas juger les gens sur la mine."

Comic or tragic, it is when Maupassant is most Norman that he is best. Norman by birth, breeding, temperament and affinities and sympathies, Norman, at bottom, he has always remained. The years of Parisian success did not have the result of making him any the more essentially Parisian, nor did his wanderings in his yacht and his excursions on African and other foreign soil transform him into even the semblance of what we nowadays style a cosmopolite. Throughout the long series of his short tales (I had the energy one day to count them, and I found that they amount to considerably over ten score) he gathers power infallibly, like Antæus, whenever he touches his mother earth. His masterpieces, the performances which laid the foundations of his subsequent great fame, what are they? *Boule-de-Suif*, subject, or at all events *mise-en-scène*, all that there is of most Norman; *La Maison Tellier*, to which may be applied precisely the same description. Only when he forsook his coign of vantage, did his hand work sometimes badly, upon material not worth the honour of his selection. There are in Maupassant at least three degrees of comparative merit—the unsurpassable, the merely excellent, the worse than worthless. Probably no other writer of his extraordinary powers has varied so greatly in respect of the result of his efforts; "efforts" being really the word in this connection, as there is plenty of internal and other evidence to show that Guy de Maupassant laboured as strenuously over his least good things as over any. Only one explanation occurs; he was deficient in artistic taste. Every quality of the great artist was Guy de Maupassant's, save one: a certain sense, as delicate as sure ("sense of the exquisite" it might be called), which will not suffer inferiority in the work's *essence*, however much, from different causes, the interest or value of the work may vary in other respects. A true sense of the exquisite is probably a moral quality in the main. And that Maupassant on his moral side was comparatively weak, is an impression that grows with careful examination of the *ensemble* of his writings, and steady reflection upon the nature of the thought and feeling which they reveal. He can not only on occasion be desperately bad; he can be bad in so many different ways! Hardly a volume of his short stories but is disfigured by a certain amount of work that for his art's sake the artist had better have left undone. It is not a question of the treatment; that, with Guy de Maupassant, in its way is always perfection, nor is it solely the choice of subject, though herein too he often enough does himself but scant justice. The fault lies in a certain unconscious dullness of touch and vulgarity of tone, which at times seem to overtake the writer like a species of moral palsy, and to render him for the nonce quite incapable of purging life from the alloy, which, precisely, is the one thing that prevents it from being art. Complicated as it is with the accidental, life cannot be transformed into art save by eliminating the accidental, so that the essential is elicited. Guy de Maupassant does not always sufficiently distinguish between accident and essence.

The alchemy of turning the lead of common existence into the gold of perfect literature is at once the great writer's secret and his reason of being. Often, indeed, has M. de Maupassant performed the miracle; but perhaps still oftener not. What was glittering specie in one place is only dry rustling leaves in another. Take *La*

Maison Tellier, for example: a less promising, nay, a more repellent subject in itself could not easily be imagined; yet Maupassant has made of it a masterpiece, if masterpiece there ever has been. The calm disregard for conventional ideas of morality, so highly moral that at times they cease to be human; the steady accuracy of touch; the searching truthfulness of tone, and in short, the command over every element of the theme: quite admirable, is here the only, the fit expression. Then the strange undercurrent of pathos; the inevitable suggestion of "the capacity for sudden innocent delights latent in natures which have lost their innocence:" that may well be left to the perfectly chosen words of Mr. Henry James. In the very descriptions of scenery there is a feeling which might vainly be sought elsewhere: "On either side of the road the green country stretched away. The colza, now in bloom, formed in spots a great carpet of undulating yellow, from which there rose a strong wholesome scent—a scent penetrating and pleasant, carried very far by the breeze. In the valley the bluebottles held up their little azure heads, which the women wished to pluck, but M. Rivet refused to stop. Then, in one place, a whole field looked as if it were sprinkled with blood, it was so crowded with poppies." This is truthful, but it is truthful in a rarely delicate way.

Now, take on the other hand a certain story—it is perhaps unnecessary to give the title—of a conversation with a police-harried female waif and stray in the Paris streets. Here everything is missed which in *La Maison Tellier* was achieved. And the more closely you examine into the reasons for the failure, the more clearly will you perceive that it is all a question of interior emotion. The moral dissection of Mme. Tellier's *pensionnaires* is performed, however deliberately, yet with no unpitying touch; whereas, somehow, the plaints of the poor girl in Paris against the boulevard, her "stony-hearted stepmother," arouse no answering echo. What was humanity in the first tale becomes mere technique in the second.

Not that Guy de Maupassant is without sufficient sympathy for the outcasts and scapegoats of existence. That is indeed one of his best traits. He who has been accused of both hardness and shortness of vision—who is supposed by certain critics never to see beneath the surface—has, in reality, at moments, a wonderful eye for the secret things that lie crushed and blighted in so many a mind and heart. Tender he hardly ever is; compassionate he can be, with the compassion that has its root in strength. It is only to be regretted that such qualities should have been so much more intermittent than regular in their effect.

Were it a question of continuing to discover specimens of Guy de Maupassant at his worst, the task, however thankless, would be easy. The most worthless stuff, perhaps, that has proceeded from his pen consists in his *tête-à-têtes* between supposed ladies of the great world, *baronnes* and *marquises* whose descent may be authentic but whose breeding and conduct are peculiar. If ladies, such as these of M. de Maupassant, are not indeed escaped inmates of the establishment of Madame Tellier, masquerading as *grandes dames*, then they ought to be, and that is all that need be said upon the subject. All the more was it tasteless and tactless on the part of M. de Maupassant to be handling this sort of matter, that he never could pretend to do it with the lightness, or brightness, or elegance of certain others. The author of *Bel-Ami* at his best is no very able painter of the brilliancies of fashionable life. And as for the subtleties of fashionable corruption—the particular delicacies and graces which, as Burke so untruly said, rob vice of "half its evils in depriving it of all its grossness"—M.

de Maupassant has neither sense to perceive nor art to reproduce. Could anything be more gross than a *marquise* of M. de Maupassant? The heroine of his appalling tale *Marroca* is ethereal by comparison. Then his many different excursions into the swamp-regions of the passionately morbid and abnormal: most of these "revelations" shock and disgust a good deal more than they horrify or surprise. With heavy tread the author goes promiscuously scattering mire. Indeed, it is not only in this connection that he impresses one as having on a pair of gigantic shooting-boots where *chaussure* of some other kind is required.

The tales of mental frenzy and aberration which from the first have been so frequent with Maupassant are no less uneven than the rest. Some are admirably good. Thus, what writer has given a stronger sense of the supernatural than is conveyed in that extraordinary story *La Peur?* It is the most perfect little piece of its kind with which I am acquainted. The intensity of dread in the closing phrases seems for the moment to seize you by the throat. But *Le Horla*, that reads like an elaborate imitation of some of the stupidest things in Edgar Poe. It is not a bit enthralling; the terror is mechanical, purely; and though of course the gradation of the mystery is ably effected (for any mere matter of technical ability Guy de Maupassant may safely be trusted), yet the mystery itself, when fully out, does not shock us in the least; as Artemus Ward might have remarked, it gives us "nary shock." The sheet being stripped off the bogy, you find with very little surprise or other emotion that he consists of a scooped-out pumpkin at the top of a long stick. It is mere spiritualism, nothing more and nothing less. In fact, on the strength of his having written *Le Horla*, doubtless the promoters of the Society of Psychical Research would be glad enough to welcome Guy de Maupassant among their adherents.

Qui Sait? is a grave and terror-stricken relation of the pranks played by a houseful of furniture which levants one night *en masse*, chairs, tables, sideboards, and the rest, without a moment's warning, stamping and trampling on the lawns and flower-beds as they go, and leaving marks of "feet" all along the gravel-paths and roads outside. More humour here, unconsciously, than in *Toine*, itself! Certain persons, I have met, deem—in still another style—*Ce Cochon de Morin* a masterpiece of fun.

For myself, I prefer the peculiar "weirdness" of *Qui Sait?*

It has been suggested that if M. de Maupassant indulged in such literary vagaries, it was perhaps because he even then felt himself to be going gradually mad. This is possible; but, despite all one's regrets, the explanation cannot be accepted as an excuse. The fact is that having hardly one of the qualities requisite for the successful treatment of eerie themes, the author of *Qui Sait?* and *Le Horla* would persist in taking them up. His very merits were against his making a success of it. The amazing directness and accuracy of the glance, the almost unparalleled fidelity of the reproducing hand; qualities invaluable in the realist, but in the mystic rather the reverse.

Not that Maupassant lacked imagination. What he lacked was what one might term moral fancy. Though he began his literary career by the publication of a small volume of verse, in divers respects he was the very opposite of a poet. In concentrating his gaze so intently upon the object, he misses the haze or halo which surrounds it. Nothing could be more characteristic, in this connection, than the piece of amatory realism entitled *Le Mur*, which comes first in the collection of Maupassant's so strongly-wrought yet so uninspired youthful poems. Here effects of moonlight among the vistas of a beautiful old park are indicated with somewhat more of precision and minuteness than most people would devote to the description of a crush of carriages in Piccadilly on a July afternoon. Had M. de Maupassant continued to apply his powers of "notation" to the sole purpose of balancing Alexandrines, it is evident that French literature would have counted one indifferent versifier the more, and one incomparable *nouvelliste* the less.

For upon the whole, incomparable he undoubtedly is as a writer of short tales. Sift out the chaff however vigorously, there yet remains much grain that is grain of gold. Surely it must suffice to a man's lasting fame to have produced but a few such masterpieces as, say, *Boule-de-Suif*, *La Maison Tellier*, *Monsieur Parent*, and *Deux Amis*.

III.

That Guy de Maupassant has not hesitated to make both "copy" and capital out of adventures of his own is plain to every sufficiently perspicacious reader. Thus the hunting and shooting stories he has produced in such abundance are not only all good, but almost all superevidently historical. Then his travels by land and sea, in Italy, Sicily, Algeria, and on board a yacht along the Mediterranean coast, have furnished him with material for no less than a trio of separate volumes.

These "wander-writings" of M. de Maupassant are broad and luminous in their general effect, and strongly marked with his interesting individuality. But here again one notes that Guy de Maupassant seems to see things solely for the purpose of describing them, where others would find reasons or at any rate pretexts for sentiment and for reflection.

Nothing in *Sur l'Eau*, or *Au Soliel*, or *La Vie Errante* is either so philosophical in thought as the *Sensations* of M. Bourget, or so rare in feeling and subtly harmonious in expression as the divers "exotisms" of Pierre Loti. What M. de Maupassant apparently considers thought, might more correctly be termed distempered brooding. His "pessimism" is so obviously of the sort that accompanies the severe headache next morning. On his boat one day off the Riviera, he falls to examining the conditions of existence. There is pain, there is poverty, there is war, there is wickedness, decline, disease, and death.

And as for the question of a hereafter, that of course is an exploded folly. The mind of the self-tormentor works and works over the dismal problem, crowded with factors that, in his arithmetic, will never accord. Sleep that night is impossible, and the next day more mental torture and unrest. Then in self-defence, as he imagines, M. de Maupassant resorts to smelling ether. . . . Having first made himself deliberately miserable, by dint of kicking against the pricks and of dwelling (*ad nauseam* indeed) upon real or fancied shortcomings of human existence, he engages by way of compensation on a course of self-destruction with drugs. Were he a "smart" woman in London or a *belle-petite* in Paris, this powerful "thinker" could hardly act with more absurdity and weakness. Surely, even before the final smash, Guy de Maupassant, like Baudelaire, must have sometimes "felt on his brow the breath of imbecility."

He is regarded, in France at least, as a representative of modern pessimism. But what is pessimism? The name and notion of the thing apparently first began to spread in connection with Schopenhauer's doctrines. Five-and-twenty years ago, it was the fashion in Paris to possess what was then denominated "la note gaie." That was the time when M. Jacques Offenbach was master of the situation. Ten or fifteen years later, every one was expected to be "pessimistic," and M. Paul Bourget was producing his first romances. All things were in the nature of the hopelessly wretched, the desperately "irreparable," the "cruelly enigmatic"; all things, save and except the fact that to write lackadaisical books gave one no end of vogue. With all this, naturally the entire spirit of the great German philosopher's teaching was ignored in favour of a mere catch-word systematically misapplied. Schopenhauer's enquiry into the conditions of the universe, so far as we are organised to cognise them, led him irresistibly to the conclusion that most things are for the worst in a singularly bad world. But in what way does it follow that every individual life should there and then cast itself bodily to the dogs? A well-known French saying insists upon the necessity and wisdom of presenting *à mauvais jeu bon visage*. And it is precisely because human existence is so doubtful and dismal at best, that each and all should strain their every nerve to make the best of it as it is. To be optimistic is a state of mind which can obviously only be that of the very unthinking, or the greatly selfish, or both in one. That optimism will never cease to have abundance of champions, seems therefore highly probable. Pessimism, on the other hand, in a certain sense is no more to be blinked by any clear-seeing eye, than is the sun's light on a cloudless noon.

In reality, however, it is optimism, not pessimism, that implies a lack of moral strength and courage. Optimism, not pessimism, is the inability or the unwillingness to recognise and to submit to the inevitable. So, though it might be laid down that optimism is as easy as being stupid, it cannot justly be said, in the language of Mr. Andrew Lang, that "pessimism is as easy as whining." The false pessimism, yes, but not the true. The pessimism of Pascal, of Schopenhauer, and other kindred souls, in the main is nothing more nor less than resignation. But certainly not in that sense has the word been interpreted of late years in France.

The strange proneness to make oneself mentally and morally ill over painful truths that one cannot possibly render less painful, was doubtless inherited by Guy de Maupassant from Gustave Flaubert. All the world knows how Flaubert taught Guy de Maupassant his trade. For seven years—usual period of an apprenticeship—the pupil elaborated essays and placed them periodically beneath the eye of the master. Apt pupil he undoubtedly was, for in the long run he outdid his mentor. In the arts of both diction and composition Maupassant eventually surpassed Flaubert as well as almost everybody else. Composition, comparatively speaking, was always a weak point with the great "hermit of Croisset." This could hardly have failed to happen, given his method of passing months over the elaboration, phrase by phrase, and word by word, of a single chapter. Unity of effect was nearly certain to be lost. Then as for style pure and simple, Flaubert in his most deliberately impersonal pieces cannot break free entirely from the rhythmical pre-occupation. His familiar (yet unwelcome) demon of romanticism lay in wait for him at the corner of every sentence, and not always did he escape without the payment of a ransom. The tendency to elation and inflation in Flaubert's magnificent prose, however desperately repressed, would of course be accounted a grave defect by the modern school of realists. Maupassant consequently gave the enemy a wide berth from the first. True, from the very nature of his temperament, he was less in danger than his elder. In him there seemed but little trace of the chivalrous, somewhat Quixotic sweep of sentiment which was at once Flaubert's weakness and his strength. Guy de Maupassant was utterly material; the very qualities which in others are moral or sentimental assumed in him a material cast. For him the difficulty was not to keep down to his mother earth, but indeed to get above it. Withal, few instances have occurred of a man discovering so soon precisely what he could hope to achieve. Promptly Maupassant discovered the direct line of his effort, and followed it deliberately and stedfastly thereafter. The small and early book of verse should be regarded mainly as an exercise in style. It was not poetry, it was scales. Then came the incomparable stories—*Boule-de-Suif*, made the success of the *Soirées de Médan*—and Guy de Maupassant was famous. Flaubert's advice and tuition must have been greatly instrumental in helping the young man to find his way; still, a personal faculty of decisiveness was evidently strong in him throughout. Possibly too, the blinker element may have played its part. It is not that Maupassant's outlook was absolutely narrow. But it was not distractingly wide. His richness lay in his strength, not his abundance. What he did he did admirably, but there is little evidence to show that he could have succeeded in anything else. His eye and his hand, rather than his mind or heart, were his great talismans: that much he has himself admitted. His gaze never failed to discern the essential characteristic—but it was often only the essential characteristic of the surface. His vision, as well as his style, was very largely a matter of sheer labour. I have heard that in the throes of composition he would write a sentence at a time, in Brobdignagian letters, with a piece of chalk, upon a blackboard, and then stand off for a while and contemplate the result. This he called "studying the physiognomy of the phrase." But, however he obtained it, undoubtedly his style (so far as it goes) is pure perfection. As has been well said by one of the most sympathetic of his critics, "every sentence is a close sequence, every epithet a paying piece." No writer beats so little about the bush; none delivers his blows more neatly, sharply, straightly, strongly. Even the comic effects, of which he is so remarkable a master, are due to precision as much as to anything else. In *Toine*, when the shrew comes in and belabours the bedridden reprobate, her husband, Maupassant writes: "Ses mains tombaient l'une après l'autre avec un bruit sourd, rapides comme les pattes d'un lapin qui bat du tambour." That is not droll in itself, it is simply exact: the comicality arises solely from the situation.

"Style"—as most French artists conceive of it—as often as not impedes rather than assists the rendering of the impression. Therefore of style in this acceptation M. de Maupassant will have none. He says himself, in his preface to *Pierre et Jean*:—"There is no need of the queer, complicated, numerous, and Chinese vocabulary which is imposed on us to-day under the name of artistic writing, to fix all the shades of thought; the right way is to distinguish with an extreme clearness all those modifications of the value of a word which come from the position it occupies. Let us have fewer nouns, verbs, and adjectives of an almost imperceptible sense, and more different phrases variously constructed, ingeniously cast, full of the science of sound and rhythm. Let us have an excellent general form rather than be collectors of rare terms." One characteristic phrase here is notable: "The right way is to distinguish with *an extreme clearness.*" That "right way" is the one M. de Maupassant has followed throughout, with regard to his outlook on the world in general as well as to his theory and practice in style. But here again one must remark that to see things, even very clearly, does not of necessity imply seeing to any great depth in them or through them.

IV.

Maupassant, no doubt, "proceeds" as directly from Flaubert as one man of such different nature can proceed from another. He regarded the author of *Trois Contes* and *La Tentation de Sainte-*

Antoine with as much filial piety as literary admiration, a fact reflecting credit and honour on him and Flaubert too. Maupassant's father, a distinguished Norman physician, was himself a Flaubert-worshipper, and apparently handed down the inclination to the son. The artistic discipleship did all the rest. There is—not to mention his preface to Flaubert's correspondence with George Sand—a stray passage in one of Maupassant's tales where, in tones of sad affection, he describes the great "stylist's" gloomy hatred of life. No doubt, had Flaubert been less of a "pessimist," Maupassant in his turn would have suffered less from the malady which his compatriots call *broyer du noir.* He would not then have begun a book of travel with these words: "J'ai quitté Paris et même la France, *parce que la tour Eiffel* finissait par m'ennuyer trop." He would not have believed that every other epoch must perforce have been preferable to that in which, as it happened, he was forced to live and move and have his being, and that every land and nation of bygone days can only have been a better land and nation than his own. Nor would he, perhaps, have written his longer books in so persistently sombre a strain. The "*illusion de l'ignoble,* that attracts so many beings"—the phrase is Guy de Maupassant's own

—really it occurs to one, as applying somewhat forcibly to himself, as one turns the pages of *Une Vie*, *Bel-Ami*, *Mont-Oriol*, *Pierre et Jean*, *Fort comme la Mort*, and *Notre Cœur*.

To moralise, I have neither authority nor inclination; still, I cannot help believing that if *Bel-Ami* and *Mont-Oriol*, in particular, may be regarded as exact presentments of contemporary society in France, then perhaps M. Guy de Maupassant's madness may have causes and excuses. *Bel-Ami* reads like nothing so much as a monstrous dream. Is it imaginable that so basely loathsome a creature as Georges Duroy—a cur as well as a scoundrel, a man of only the lowest degree of intelligence and most vulgar type of physical good looks—should start at page 1 from the gutter, and at page 441 be the husband of a charming young wife, the lover of every desirable woman that he has met, the owner of millions of money (francs, to be sure, but that is bad enough), and moreover a person of political as well as social power and prestige? The book is so wonderfully well done in its way—so full of colour, bustle, and ingenious and interesting detail—that, as one reads, it casts a sort of spell upon the mind. Only later does the glamour fade, upon reflection. Casanova, Duroy's superior along not dissimilar lines, didn't, after all, make so brilliant a success of his existence; and that at a period when in European pleasure-seeking circles licence ran high enough, assuredly, for anything or anybody. Barry Lyndon "scored" well enough from the material point of view, but he met with a certain amount of unconquerable aversion to the very end. Some few honest persons held out against him. It is true that Georges Duroy, to use the French colloquial expression, is "dragged through the mud" in his absence by everyone who knows him. The very people, however, who give him the worst character "behind his back," submit most willingly to his ascendancy when he is present. Many others, moreover (mostly women), under all circumstances swear by him.

Now, Paris in the present generation is not exactly the home of all the virtues. Yet it seems on the face of things impossible that the Paris of reality can be the Paris of *Bel-Ami*. A whole book crowded with *dramatis personæ*, and not a single honest or even amiable character among them all,—for Mme. Walter, at her best, is weak and foolish, and as to her daughter Suzanne, finally married to Duroy, we are somehow led to conclude that from her, later on, anything in nature or out of it may be expected: yes, surely it is a nightmare; it can't be real human life. Did such a state of things actually exist, sulphur and brimstone would be too good for it. Merely one more instance of the tricks played upon M. de Maupassant by his ineradicable *illusion de l'ignoble!* Life, no doubt, is full of Georges Duroys; but they must have in them something more than Georges Duroy had, either from the point of view of brains or that of feeling, before they may hope to mount as he did from the lowest to the topmost round. A certain height they may well attain to. But there they always find a check,—not a little, perhaps, to their own astonishment. For with the peculiar kind of local unintelligence that naturally accompanies ill-will, they cannot understand that the greatest degree of success necessitates positively the possession of moral sentiments of a certain order. Discussions concerning the probable virtues and vices of Napoleon Bonaparte, for example, are idle. He *must* have had it in him to be high-souled, if not large-hearted, seeing that without wings it is not possible to soar. But *Bel-Ami*, like other characters by the same author, is in the main a revelation of M. de Maupassant's weak side. It is the Bel-Amis in his work that show where the shoe pinches. Maupassant, in all material respects so keen, so perspicacious, with regard to moral questions, impresses one often as actually dull.

Mont-Oriol is less disagreeable than *Bel-Ami* only because in certain ways there is less of it. The "personages" are fewer, the scene of action more restricted. Its subject has been indicated perspicuously thus "A gentleman, if he happen to be a low animal, is liable to love a lady very much less if she presents him with a pledge of their affection." The lady and gentleman in question, it should be added, are united in bonds of wedlock with a couple of other people. Still, we are made to feel that Paul Brétigny, the "low animal," is not such a very bad fellow after all. He is simply a "product," like the rest of us. Circumstances have made him what he is. If this be indeed the case—if determination, in other words, be really the mainspring of our system—it is to be regretted that the circumstances surrounding the Paul Brétignys should not be different.

Pleasure is found in turning to another novel of Guy de Maupassant's, his first, and also perhaps his best. At all events, *Une Vie* is in every respect preferable to *Mont-Oriol* and *Bel-Ami*. Maupassant was fresh from Flaubert's influence when he wrote it, and no doubt it seems a little like a *pendant* to *Madame Bovary*, that worst of novels to choose as model. *Une Vie* can well stand, however, on literary feet of its own. But for a few passages and pages, not amounting to a chapter altogether, where, with such infelicitous effect, M. de Maupassant has violated the first principles of artistic reticence—has described, and described brutally, instead of merely indicating or suggesting—the book would not fall far short of a *chef d'œuvre.* There is a hidden soul of tenderness and sympathy in it, which enhances strangely the (even thus early) splendid power of execution, the assured, serried perfection of technique. A poor woman's whole lifetime of unmerited pain and grief, to be told in minute detail, and yet without one syllable in excess : difficult problem for a literary beginner, yet which M. de Maupassant triumphantly solved. Freely one may confess that one likes *Une Vie* better than the rest of M. de Maupassant's long books, unless perchance an exception be made in favour of *Pierre et Jean.*

This, by common consent, within its limits is a very admirable production. Shorter, more condensed, and slighter in theme, it is more in the nature of a short story elaborately worked up. And it, also, shows but little of Maupassant's brutality. A thing greatly to Maupassant's credit is that the characters he handles with most kindness are those of simple folk, in whom the capacity for feeling pain is in an inverse ratio to the will or power of inflicting it. Poor Jeanne de Lamare in *Une Vie* is one such, she whose heart is so soft that all things in a world hard as this can only bruise it. Mme. Roland in *Pierre et Jean* is another. And always—even as it were in defiance of his own emotion—Maupassant has the little fine, sought-for word that curiously denotes and that sharply specialises, instead of leaving things in the state of happy, facile vagueness so dear to the "optimist" heart. One can feel that he feels for his Mme. Roland. Yet, when wishing to suggest that she has a gentle nature, he alludes to her "âme tendre *de caissière*. "Caissières" in French cafés and shops lead a ruminating sort of existence, that predisposes them to dreamy gentleness, not unlike that of big-eyed creatures which browse all day in peaceful fields. An easy mechanical occupation has effects which remove a nature with any degree of good in it further and further away from bitterness and agitation and guile. Beyond doubt this fact would be patent to an eagerly close observer, and thus is justified Guy de Maupassant's "âme tendre de caissière." It might be deemed either meaningless or merely fanciful, but as a matter of fact it is not. These, doubtless, are trifling points, but of just such trifles is made up the writer's art. The epithets of Guy de Maupassant, indeed, like those of every other first-rate French writer of this time, are a separate study in themselves. It has, however, occurred to me more than once that only with a public so perceptive as the French can it be possible to venture on such infinitely fine shades of expression with any hope of being understood. That which in France even the average reader will hail as a felicity, in England will be thought an affectation. "A Paris, on se comprend à demi-mot: quelque fois même avant. Pourvu que la pensée des autres soit à peine indiquée, nous la complétons." That is true, M. Jean Richepin; but true of Paris alone. M. Jules Lemaître, in describing one of the heroines of the author who is the subject of this sketch, speaks of her eyes like "faded flowers." Possibly that most lovely touch would not be lost on some British readers. But when using a figure that is not a whit more unacceptable or unpleasing to the French taste, the critic of the *Débats* goes on to speak of the *nez souriant* of the lady, he swims out of English ken altogether. *Nez souriant* in French is exquisite; "a smiling nose" in English is worse than absurd. Pray allow me to consider the fact as simply showing that a certain quaint grace of thought is like the fairies that won't approach running waters: it declines entirely to cross the Channel. If you cannot recognise that noses as well as eyes may have their expression, life isn't quite the same to you as it is to certain others.

Is the body really all in all? for if so, when the body begins to decay, the soul must sink within us, and so will we die a hundred deaths before our time. If *Fort comme la Mort* have any moral, beyond the general gloom of its hopeless sadness, that is it. The book, by the way, marks the beginning of a second literary manner in Guy de Maupassant. He who had previously scoffed at the very notion of "psychology"; he who had adduced, as, *e. g.*, in the preface to *Pierre et Jean*, many excellent and most plausible arguments to show why psychology and nonsense must be well-nigh synonymous terms; here makes a determined effort to be psychological himself. If he does not completely succeed in the attempt, that, under the circumstances, is scarcely a matter for surprise. After so long remaining upon the surface, it was not easy all at once to find his way about beneath it. But the mere desire to study actions less and motives more should be accounted as righteousness in any "realist." Two-thirds of *Fort comme la Mort* are taken up with Maupassant's usual accumulation of small though highly characteristic exterior detail. This forms as it were a background, against which the purely moral interest of the final portion of the book stands out in greatly enhanced relief.

Than this volume, no stronger sermon has been delivered in denunciation of the essential hollowness of all that appertains to the "lust of the flesh, the lust of the eye, the pride of life." To "conclude" is not the novelist's business, though it may be that of the preacher; yet certainly there may be such a thing as not concluding enough. We have, at all events, some right to demand that the writer shall conclude in his own mind. Now somehow, with regard to *Fort comme la Mort*, we feel that even in his own mind M. de Maupassant has not concluded. He has seen, perhaps even he has felt, but a vague misery and distress is all his observations have brought him; he has not taken the necessary further steps of deducing from personal experiences of pain a general theory of acceptance and melioration. From Shakespeare's "limbecks foul as hell within" he has not distilled the magic elixir of resignation in default of happiness or of content. Thrice blessed he who has!

Notre Cœur acquires a special interest of melancholy through being, if I mistake not, the last printed work by Guy de Maupassant. It appeared serially, as every one will remember, in the pages of the *Deux Mondes*, which secular sheets, by the way, must have thrilled in holy horror at so singularly "modern" an intrusion. At hazard I open the volume, and my eye lights on a casual phrase: "Il était torturé, car il l'aimait." Is love, then, with M. de Maupassant, necessarily equivalent to torture? Small wonder if a brain so affected has ended by going wrong. There is a greater effort at mere brilliancy, perhaps, in *Notre Cœur* than in any of the preceding novels. The social tone is more marked at once and more felicitous. Michèle de Burne, that human mermaid, that monster of mean selfishness and cold perversion, has at least more of the exterior marks of a woman of the world than one is used to in the heroine of Guy de Maupassant. She, at all events, does not belong to the race of the *baronnes* and *marquises*—though no better at bottom and perhaps a good deal worse. If you haven't principle, have honour; if you haven't honour, have soul; if you haven't soul, have heart; if you haven't heart, have passion. This woman has neither passion, heart, soul, honour, principle, nor aught else. Cunning she has, and a certain mundane polish, and a vanity that is devouring; she gloats over her physical beauty in secret, loves it too much to love any human being half as well, and lives only to cultivate it night and day. Given, on the other hand, a man of anxious artistic temperament and of relaxed uncertain will, certain it is that contact with such a creature can mean only wretchedness for him. And so poor André Mariolle finds it in the book.

Desinit in piscem applies to *Notre Cœur* more than to any other of Maupassant's novels. It, indeed, trails off so nervelessly, so feebly, so incongruously, all the living interest seeming to ooze out of it at the end like the sawdust out of a pin-pricked doll, that in reading it one is reminded irresistibly of the affection which even then must have been at work upon its author's brain.

V.

A powerful and brilliant if not great literary artist: this Guy de Maupassant undoubtedly was, and it is lamentable that with perhaps long years of continued life before him, one should be speaking of him in the past. His own life—setting aside all vulgar gossip, and judging solely from what he has allowed us to know—was weaker and more unsuccessful, as to its "style" and its "composition," than any other of his works. The greater the genius the more elements it must contain that tend towards moral and often physical disruption. One cannot be "rich" without being complex, and one cannot be complex without being more or less "potential" for evil as well as good. But (and in this "but" how much there is of virtue!) the greater, more general, more developed and assured the ability of the artist, the more successfully will he hold in check those tendencies that threaten to destroy him. Chamfort said, though not exactly in these words, "My passions are to me what his acids are to the chemist. If he pours them away, how carry on his experiments?" The answer is that whatever else the chemist may do with them, he at least does not dine and sup on them, and so get poisoned. The superior man is not merely single or even twofold. Indeed, even Pierre Loti's "Nous avons en nous un tas d'invididus différents, sans compter les animaux," does not completely cover the ground. What we really "have within us" is a very regiment of forces of various nature. But that regiment must have a leader, or life can but end in miserable defeat. An instance of the gifted man whose regiment was not well led is Guy de Maupassant. On the other hand Goethe—to select him as the very greatest—may stand as representative of those whose powers have been placed under due control. And he, had he known the author of *Fort comme la Mort*, doubtless would have drawn from the history of this ill-starred genius a moral very similar to that he draw from the history of Torquato Tasso.

THE POET VERLAINE.

I.

WERE I called on to declare in a word what I think the keynote of Verlaine, I should reply—it is to be found in his peculiar thrill of *grief*. "You have invented a new shudder," wrote Victor Hugo to Baudelaire. What Verlaine has invented is a new shade of woe.

In the attempt to define in its full distinctness and uniqueness the particular, mournful, world-weary, world-wounded thrill which is the Verlaine *leit-motiv*, recourse must be had to negatives. It is not wistfully cold and pure like the melancholy of De Vigny; not raging and wailing by turns like the angry sorrow of Musset; not deliberately and calmly desperate like the pessimism of Leconte de Lisle; not quivering continually at the precise point between tears and smiles like the pathos of Heine, and not consistently, logically agonising like the world-horror of Leopardi. It is something less material than even the least material of these. . . . Something imperceptibly faint and slight, like the liliputian wreath of vapour that might rise from hot tears shed silently one by one in secret; something throbbing in a sort of reproachful dumbness of amaze, a dulness and deadness of pain, like some very frail and small creature crushed bleeding to the ground by a big and brutal force or being that it cannot rightly understand. . .

In the Jardin des Plantes at Paris, in a fine grassy enclosure, is a group of tiny animals, the smallest antelopes known. They will come, about the size of so many cats, close behind their low wire grating, and stand and doubtfully gaze up at you with enormous liquid eyes. And such is the effect of their littleness, their timorousness, their almost absurd delicacy—so small, so delicate, those little, little hoofs, those little tender limbs, those fragile fawn-coloured sides, that little humid twitching muzzle; so small, and yet so keenly, tremulously perceptive and so intensely sensitive; so little, yet all alive and quivering with nerves; so small, so weak, so helpless, and apparently so unfitted for aught except to apprehend; such minute atoms and specks of sentient being, so lost amid a universe's vast incomprehensibility—

that my heart has been smitten to look upon those miniature living things, with the quite inordinate fraility of their body and the disproportionate bigness of their eyes.

Symbols or suggestions of humanity's every aspect may, one fancies, be discovered in animal creation. And I think those antelopes are symbols of a state of soul rare enough among men, and yet too frequent. A somewhat similar combination of hopeless powerlessness to resist with the most unbounded capacity to suffer ("As-tu réfléchi combien nous sommes organisés pour le malheur?" Flaubert wrote to George Sand) is reflected in Verlaine's verse.

> " Le ciel est, par-dessus le toit,
> Si bleu, si calme!
> Un arbre, par-dessus le toit,
> Balance sa palme.
>
> " La cloche dans le ciel qu'on voit
> Doucement tinte;
> Un oiseau sur l'arbre qu'on voit
> Chante sa plainte.
>
> " Mon Dieu, mon Dieu, la vie est là,
> Simple et tranquille;
> Cette paisible rumeur-là
> Vient de la ville.
>
> " —Qu'as-tu fait, ô toi que voilà,
> Pleurant sans cesse;
> Dis, qu'as-tu fait, toi que voilà,
> De ta jeunesse?"

To my perhaps excessive sensibility, there is about that little piece, with the melting silvery softness and sweetness of its opening and the broken suddenness and sternness of the closing apostrophe to the sinner by his soul, a sort of breath, as it were, of haggard horror. Intensity, so profound as to be almost quiescent; despair too great for words, and best expressed by the choking abruptness of a sob.

In these lines, too, that follow, what mournfulness of brooding, and what strange imaginative effect:—

> "Je ne sais pourquoi
> Mon esprit amer
> D'une aile inquiète et folle vole sur la mer.
> Tout ce qui m'est cher
> D'une aile d'effroi
> Mon amour le couve au ras des flots. Pourquoi, pourquoi?"

The above stanza for mere workmanship is very striking. The extraordinary prolongation of the Alexandrine: "D'une aile inquiète et folle vole sur la mer," which suggests the protracted sonorous unfurling of the wave upon the beach or the heavy tardy winging of the gull against the wind, is effected, technically speaking, by the use of the two lengthened "a" sounds in "aile" and "inquiète," and of the "o" sound in the rhyming "folle" and "vole." Here it may be noted that Verlaine makes somewhat frequent, and always most felicitous use of casually recurrent rhymes within the verse. Another characteristic of Verlaine's manner is his employment of irregular nine-foot, eleven-foot, and thirteen-foot metres, giving results of lightness, fluidity, and softness not to be obtained with the artificial, Versailles-park trimness of such forms as the classic Alexandrine for example. In this as in divers similar particulars, Verlaine's art, by reason of its varied originality and ingenuity, would well repay a greater amount of study than the limits of this paper will allow.

Among Verlaine's "pièces de tristesse" the following is perhaps the best known:—

"Les sanglots longs
Des violons
De l'automne
Blessent mon cœur
D'une langueur
Monotone.

"Tout suffocant
Et blême quand
Sonne l'heure,
Je me souviens
Des jours anciens
Et je pleure,

"Et je m'en vais
Au vent mauvais

Qui m'emporte
De ci, de là,
Pareil à la,
Feuille morte."

Who, walking in some silent wood in late November, has not been conscious, if for an instant only, of the scent, faint yet sharp and fresh although so eloquent of decay, that breathes from matted heaps of fallen leaves at the foot of the denuded trees? Some such fragrance seems to hang upon the quaintness of those lines, with their tremulous indecision of design so justly and subtly corresponding to the undefined sadness of the emotion.

In days comparatively distant Verlaine occasionally could indulge without admixture of acerbity or grief in the delicate, graceful lyric strain constituting one of the chief notes of his genius. For sweetness, simplicity, and freshness, the little piece that follows is like the thrush's silver trill: —

"La lune blanche
Luit dans les bois;
De chaque branche
Part une voix
Dans la ramée . . .

O bien aimée!

"L'étang reflète
—Profond miroir—
La silhouette
Du saule noir
Où le vent pleure . . .
Rêvons, c'est l'heure.

"Un vaste et tendre
Apaisement
Semble descendre
Du firmament
Que l'astre irise . . .
C'est l'heure exquise."

How lovely, too, is just this snatch :—

"Avant que tu ne t'en ailles,
Pâle étoile du matin,
Mille cailles
Chantent, chantent dans le thym."

But this early brightness of his song was soon to be lost in the black bitterness expressed from one of the most tragic and terrible—morally speaking—of all poetic lives.

II.

. . . What causes for Verlaine's sadness, for Verlaine's perplexity, complexity, perversion? . . . To a sympathetic comprehension they are apparent clearly enough. The, so usual, domestic misunderstandings—the material difficulties of existence, hard to all, but to one constituted like this, how much more distracting, more degrading, more destructive: is it strange if Paul Verlaine, poor in purse, sad in soul, and grieving for a "loved and lost Lenore" (if not materially lost, yet lost in the spirit, which was worse); strange, if he "sought surcease of sorrow" and the semblance at least of sympathy intellectual and artistic among those Bohemian tavern *coteries* which have long played so great, so exorbitant a part in Parisian life? He sought sympathy, and he found—what was inevitable: coarseness, baseness, envy, malice, and all the other qualities presented by humanity in conglomoration. Through weeks, and months, and years, he sat and listened to the clacking of the poisonous tongues, and to the crackling of the thorns under the pot; and "assisted" daily, nightly, at the vile constant dragging downward of all things not naturally rooted in the mud. "Rooted in the mud" is a term that might finally have been appropriately applied to himself. Contamination, in a case like his, was certain. And the effects on him of such contamination were bound to be especially disastrous. By his own admission in his verse, he sank low. Lower even, if conceivable, than any of his "Bohemian" accomplices.

It is a striking psychological fact, on which all thinkers must have pondered, that extremes of evil in natures of a certain exquisite type should lie so close beside extremes of good. The worst iniquity is often, as Baudelaire's verse for instance forcibly suggests, nothing more than the logical action in the last resort of an excessive ideality deprived of all exterior aliment and thrown back violently upon itself. Verlaine profoundly touches this point in a line of his allegorical poem entitled—all too significantly—*Crimen Amoris*. In a palace blazing with silk and gold, at Ecbatane in Asia, to the sound of Mohammedan melodies strange and strident, a band of juvenile Satans "font litière aux sept péchés de leurs cinq sens." The demons (demons, remember, are angels degraded) desire vainly to break away from the Evil to which they are attached, but which at heart they abhor. And one, youngest and brightest of them all, despairingly exclaims:—

> "Nous avons tous trop souffert, anges et hommes,
> *De ce conflit entre le Pire et le Mieux!*"

Yes, evidently, a soul is like a blade. The more purely, finely tempered, the more in danger of losing its edge. What less Verlaine-like existence—what, to all exterior appearances, less Verlaine-like character—than that of Nathaniel Hawthorne? Yet see how thoroughly, in his tale *The Artist of the Beautiful*, the American psychologist comprehends and how capitally expresses this truth, so saddening if rightly considered, the last crowning cruelty among the hardships attaching to genius's earthly lot: "He [the Artist] abandoned himself to habits from which it might have been supposed that the mere delicacy of his organisation would have availed to secure him. But, when the ethereal portion of a man of genius is obscured, the earthly part assumes an influence the more uncontrollable, because the character is now thrown off the balance to which Providence had so nicely adjusted it; and which, in coarser natures, is adjusted by some other method." Paul Verlaine, like Owen Harland in that story, "abandoned himself to habits from which it might have been supposed," &c. Also like François Villon, his prototype four hundred years ago. In Verlaine's life, as in Villon's, the same complication is presented of essential moral loveliness with the most lamentable ignominy of circumstance. To say "conduct," in reference to such bruised reeds swirling in the brook or dead leaves whirling in the wind as are the Villons and Verlaines, one feels would not be just.

For all the degradation, however, of this Parisian *brasserie* sphere which for years was Paul Verlaine's, it has within the limits of the present generation attracted and detained genius, not his alone. Men, with whom in times not so very long past the poet has sat imbibing *chopes* of Munich beer, and hardly money enough among the lot to be quite certain of "settling" at the end of the evening, have come since to be the rulers of France:—

> "Vous voici rois de France! A votre tour!
> (Rois à plusieurs d'une France postiche) . . ."

is how Verlaine has apostrophised them in his verse. Other men, of the erst beerhouse frequenters, are now the editors of great leading "organs." Others, again, authors of books the world has read, or painters of pictures the world has rushed to see. Never has French society, in these respects, been more Balzacian than during the past twenty or thirty years. But what has mainly impressed the poet of *Sagesse* and *Amour* in connection with these *parvenu* associates of his youth is the vanity and insincerity of most "successful" art, the backstairs and dirty-dish-washing loathsomeness of most "successful" politics, the vile venality and time-service of most journalism of the "influential" type. . . . The course of events, public and private, the development of others' character and his own, and the general spectacle of the "civilization" circumambient—these, the divers factors of a painful and perhaps insoluble world-problem, have each and all had their effect of misanthropy on Verlaine. Man delights him not, nor woman (the beerhouse variety of the species) neither:—

> "*Ces femmes!* Dis les gaz, et l'horreur identique
> Du mal partout, du laid toujours sur tes chemins;
> Et dis l'Amour et dis encor la Politique
> Avec du sang déshonoré d'encre à leurs mains!"

Another instance of the deepness of his "political" scorn:—that which most interests him in relation with the phenomenon named Louise Michel, is the lady's high Christian ideal of justice, on the one hand, as contrasted with, on the other, the peculiar characteristics of the persons said and supposed to "govern." The "Ballade en l'honneur de Louise Michel" has a fine stirring ring. It thus concludes:—

"Gouvernements de maltalent,
Mégathérium ou baccile,
Soldat brut, robin insolent,
Ou quelque compromis fragile,
Géant de boue aux pieds d'argile—
Tout cela son courroux chrétien
L'écrase d'un mépris agile.
Louise Michel est très bien.

Envoi.

Citoyenne! Votre évangile
On meurt pour! C'est l'honneur! Eh bien,
Loin des Taxil et des Basile
Louise Michel est très bien."

III.

If in the art, literature, politics, and society of France since 1870 Verlaine has found but little to appease his nature's inner cravings for fitness ethic and æsthetic, neither have the exterior aspects of Paris itself brought unquestioning delight to his mind or eye:—

"La 'grande ville.' Un tas criard de pierres blanches
Où rage le soleil comme en pays conquis.
Tous les vices ont leur tanière, les exquis
Et les hideux, dans ce désert de pierres blanches."

Such are the distasteful thoughts with which the "décor" of outward Paris inspires him.

The theme, however, is not always treated by Verlaine in this moralising vein. White streets, gay parks, bustling suburban fêtes, busy faubourgs, banal *banlieue*, the varied Parisian scenery familiar in Coppée's verse, De Nittis's and Béraud's paintings, Forain's sketches and aquarelles; there is much of this in Verlaine, done with a smartness, brightness, vividness of touch quite delightful. Instantaneous photographs, only artistic; like this, of a corner at a fair:—

> "Le tréteau qu'un orchestre emphatique secoue
> Grince sous les grands pieds du maigre baladin,
> Qui harangue, non sans finesse et sans dédain,
> Les badauds piétinant devant lui dans la boue."

And now this *effet de faubourg*:—

> "Le bruit des cabarets, la fange du trottoir
> Les platanes déchus s'effeuillant dans l'air noir,
> L'omnibus, ouragan de ferrailles et de boues,
> Qui grince, mal assis entre ses quatre roues,
> Et roule ses yeux verts et rouges lentement,
> Les ouvriers allant au club, tout en fumant
> Leur brûle-gueule au nez des agents de police,
> Toits qui dégouttent, murs suintants, pavé qui glisse,
> Bitume défoncé, ruisseaux comblant l'égout,
> Voila ma route—*avec le paradis au bout.*"

In passing let me note how readily, for all his

intense Parisianism, modernism, impressionism, Verlaine turns to allegory that simplest, yet profoundest, of poetic moral effects. He is naturally allegorical, like Baudelaire, Hawthorne, Poe.

. . . This flat, sordid *paysage de banlieue* :—

> " Vers Saint-Denis, c'est bête et sale la campagne.
> C'est pourtant là qu'un jour j'emmenai ma compagne.
> Nous étions de mauvaise humeur et querellions.
> Un plat soleil d'été tartinait ses rayons
> Sur la plaine sêchée ainsi qu'une rôtie.
> C'était pas trop après le Siège : une partie
> Des ' Maisons de Campagne ' gisait à terre encor,
> D'autres se relevaient comme on hisse un décor,
> Et des obus tout neufs encastrés aux pilastres
> Portaient écrit autour : ' Souvenir des Désastres.' "

IV.

Of Verlaine's sense for love in the abstract, meaning, in the concrete, woman—and as everyone knows who *quà* critic knows anything, 'tis the nature and degree of his sense for love that give the truest measure of the poet—I shall only say that it is at once most delicate, most exquisite and most unhappily questioning and revolted. The core of animalism in even the feminine nature is odiously apparent to Verlaine's sense. Vigny's line, so shocking in its ferocious physiologism of denunciation :—

> "La femme, enfant malade et *douze fois impur.* . . ."

that line, that hideous line, haunts his imagination and taints, with both the fact and the allegory it involves, all the loveliness, all the superdelicacy of his passion for—

> "L'or des cheveux, l'azur des yeux, la fleur des chairs."

The cruel faculty of the analyst is Verlaine's : the painfully piercing glance, painful alike to him and to his victim, that gazes half-involuntarily upon the nudeness of the poor flawed stigmatised clay :—

> "Tu m'as, ces pâles jours d'automne blanc, fait mal,
> *A cause de tes yeux où fleurit l'animal.* . . ."

Never, to Verlaine, is woman so divine as when her animal nature sinks into latency, quiescence, and may, for one moment, be lost to his perception :—

> "Beauté des femmes, leur faiblesse et ces mains pâles
> Qui font souvent le bien et peuvent tout le mal,
> Et ces yeux, *ou plus rien ne reste d'animal*
> Que juste assez pour dire 'assez' aux fureurs mâles. . ."

Verlaine could write, and, doubtless, often think :—

> " . . . . heure sainte
> *Ou non*, qu'importe à votre extase, Amour et Chair?"—

but in moments when, true to the essential Platonism of his nature, he rises into purer regions than those haunted by a Mendès or Baudelaire, what he thinks, and writes, is the following :—

> " Va, l'étreinte jalouse et *le spasme obsesseur*
> Ne valent pas un long baiser, même qui mente. . . ."

His disgust at the brutality of material love well expresses itself in a line of his sonnet " Dandysme " :—

> " Pauvres gens que les gens ! Mourir pour Célimène,
> Epouser Angélique ou venir de nuit chez
> Agnès et *la briser*. . . ."

Carnality (never, by the way, more ruthless, more sheer, than when completely and most "respectably" legal: M. Filon, the French critic, expressed acutely an undeniable truth when he wrote of " la sensualité légale, cette chose essentiellement anglaise "), carnality, *per se*, Verlaine abhors. To him it seems a loathsome thing, the slimy slug upon the plant:—

> " Tel un pur, un sublime amour,
> *Qu'eût étreint la luxure infâme. . . .*"

But if carnality pure and simple repels him, depravity in its more refined forms exercises a quite morbid attraction for his spirit. Take as proof his *Fêtes Galantes.* Redolent it is, of all possible loveliness of sin; all imaginable grace, charm, force, terror, diabolism, delight of the thoroughly corrupt. A tiny wreath, woven with delicate, delicious art, of the rarest, subtlest, sweetest flowers of passionate aberrance and unhealth, insinuating—so strongly!—on the sense, the languor, torpor, from which there may be no awaking. The fullest essence is herein, of that dangerous eighteenth-century compound of sensuality the most determined, refinement the most delightful, intelligence the most vivid, elegance the most extreme. Twenty little pieces, as cunningly coquettish, as scientifically suggestive, of all by which depravity may be, has been, rendered stronger than love and than death, as one fancies the bewitching patches were that showed black upon the pulp-whiteness of the Dubarry's nude skin. Twenty little pieces of verse, steeped to the lips in the French *dix-*

huitième siècle's perfumed and gilded putrescence. Yet, by a touch here and there, as of an organ note now and again among the "pleasing" of flutes and lutes, is made to be felt the poet's own occasional interior thrill at the thought of the essential horror underlying this "gallantry" and these "fêtes." For example, the two typical young lovers, in their satins and their ruffles, and their courtly high-heeled shoes, escorting thorugh the decorous old park two glittering belles, all smiles, all furbelows, all freshness. . . The youths eye the daintiness of the ladies' attire, and note furtively the provoking, distracting, half-display, half-concealment of a score of secret charms. Each little incident of the scene and hour—the leafy contact of an overhanging bough, the hum of some presumptuous insect—provides a pretext for *rapprochements* which the young men seem to dread, while the belles more boldly desire :—

" Parfois aussi le dard d'un insecte jaloux
Inquiétait le col des belles sous les branches,
Et c'était des éclairs soudains de nuques blanches,
Et ce régal comblait nos jeunes yeux de fous.

" Le soir tombait, un soir équivoque d'automne :
Les belles, *se pendant rêveuses à nos bras.*
Dirent alors des mots si spécieux, tout bas,
Que notre âme depuis ce temps tremble et s'étonne ! "

Oh, how admirably is Verlaine's own attitude of soul there expressed, as, whilst succumbing to the "*specious* words, low-whispered" of all which is most delicate among the lusts of the flesh, he yet feels that wild strange thrill of doubt and terror and amaze,—the throbbing of the breast of the bird, when it finds its foot glued irrecoverably to the twig! . . .

"... Fardée et peinte comme au temps des bergeries,
Frêle parmi les nœuds énormes de rubans,
Elle passe, sous les ramures assombries,
Dans l'allée où verdit la mousse des vieux bancs
Avec mille façons et mille afféteries
Qu'on garde d'ordinaire aux perruches chéries.
Sa longue robe à queue est bleue, et l'éventail
Qu'elle froisse en ses doigts fluets aux larges bagues
S'égaie en des sujets érotiques, si vagues
Qu'elle sourit, tout en rêvant à maint détail
—Blonde en somme. Le nez mignon avec la bouche
Incarnadine, grasse, et divine d'orgueil
Inconscient.—D'ailleurs plus fine que la mouche
Qui ravive l'éclat un peu niais de l'œil."

That precious little sonnet, a *Watteau retouché à l'eau-forte*, comprises the whole eighteenth-century Frenchwoman, most efficient of stalking-horses behind which the Devil has gone hunting for souls. Comment upon the art of the thing would be useless. No one susceptible of perceiving its dainty *pimpant* grace has need that the same should be expounded, whilst to others, what amount of explanation could convey the entire effect.

See how, in a further piece, the poet curiously, keenly, but not unkindly, stands contemplating Colombine—little head, no heart, appetite, perhaps, but no real passion, and in a word, all small, sure, shrewd, cold, hard, *self-love*—as she leads her pack of danglers a merry dance:—

> " Léandre le sot,
> Pierrot qui d'un saut
> De puce
> Franchit le buisson,
> Cassandre sous son
> Capuce,
> Arlequin aussi. . . ."

Touched to seriousness for one moment, the moralist inquires of the mute fatefulness of the stars:—

> " Fatidique cours des astres
> Oh! dis-moi vers quels
> Mornes ou cruels
> Désastres
>
> " L'implacable enfant
> Preste et relevant
> Ses jupes,
> La rose au chapeau
> Conduit son troupeau
> De dupes ?"

Yet even Colombine—even this typical coquette —is not without the faintest shadow of a flutter, sometimes, in the place where might be situated her heart :—

> " Colombine rêve, surprise,
> De sentir un cœur dans la brise
> Et d'entendre en son cœur des voix."

V.

. . . And so with Paul Verlaine, the fatal process went on. . . . From temptation to excess, excess to satiety, satiety to disgust; all, all in love, all love and every kind of love, is hollow utterly, utterly false :—

> " Toutes les amours de la terre
> Laissent au cœur du délétère
> Et de l'affreusement amer ;
> Fraternelles et conjugales,
> Paternelles et filiales,
> Civiques et nationales,
> Les charnelles, les idéales,
> Toutes ont la guèpe et le ver. . . ."

From disgust finally to remorse :—

> " J'aurais dû passer dans l'odeur et le frais
> De l'arbre et du fruit sans m'arrêter jamais ;
> Le ciel m'a puni . . . J'aurais dû, j'aurais dû !"

Till at last the poet turns him away from the vanities of earthly passion, and seeks a refuge in the pity, and the pardon, and the tenderness ineffable, that some declare and perhaps believe and feel to be existent within the depths of a heaven, to others a blank and void.

> " . . . Il faut n'être pas dupe en ce farceur de monde
> Où le bonheur n'a rien d'exquis et d'alléchant,
> S'il n'y frétille un peu de pervers et d'immonde,
> Et pour n'être pas dupe il faut être méchant."

Yes, but :—

> " Bien de n'être pas dupe dans ce monde d'une heure.
> Mais pour ne l'être pas durant l'éternité,
> *Ce qu'il faut à tout prix qui règne et qui demeure,*
> *Ce n'est pas la méchanceté, c'est la bonté.*"

Indeed, throughout the thickest of his impiety Verlaine had not been without some latent sense of grace :—

> " Mais sans doute, et moi j'inclinerais fort à le croire,
> Dans quelque coin bien discret et sûr de ce cœur même
> Il avait gardé comme qui dirait la mémoire
> D'avoir été ces petits enfants que Jésus aime. . ."

and the day came, when under circumstances of great disgrace, affliction, and despair, he seems actually to have been penetrated with the " peace that passeth all understanding" (as indeed, anyone not personally possessing it must confess that it does). But such is the strange complexity of the artist nature, that to it the finest, noblest, highest emotions, as well as, perchance, the darkest and worst, must be always themes, for emotional and artistic treatment and expression, rather than direct, absolute, genuine sentiments in themselves. The artist has but one genuine sentiment, and that is: Art. A doubt therefore subsists as to the completeness of this conversion of Verlaine's. And such doubt becomes, to a mind possessed of any critical acumen, an almost certainty when one finds Verlaine claiming the right to produce "*Parallèlement*," as he calls it, by way of title to one of his more recent volumes, verse devoted to emotions of religion on the one hand, and emotions of the senses on the other: a striking instance of the wish poetically to serve those two irreconcilable masters, God and the World. Thus art, plainly, is stronger in Verlaine's breast than faith.

He has lived for his art alone, and by reason of his art he must die; because, full of art, he is void of many things else. Void of broad general humanity, void of the deeper world-wisdom, void of the eloquence most penetrating and profound that coming from the heart goes to the heart not of the time merely but of all time, and speaks, a lofty Voice, along the ages.

No great poet, no world-poet, is Paul Verlaine. But the exquisite, delightful, diseased, lacerated poet of a morbid *élite*. In the main, however, a touching figure, with the intensity of his emotion, elevation of his impulse, and fatal weakness of his will. Poor knight-errant, bruised and broken, with that headpiece of "singing gold," that flaming Nessus's "tunic" of grief and sin, and the red blood from his breast raining down upon the "azure ground" of his illusions :—

> "J'étais né pour plaire à toute âme un peu fière.
>
> . . . .
>
> J'étais, je suis né pour plaire aux nobles âmes,
> Pour les consoler un peu d'un monde impur,
> *Cimier d'or chanteur et tunique de flammes,*
> *Moi, le Chevalier qui saigne sur azur !*"

Yes, poor wandering, worsted knight, wandering and worsted and woeful and utterly downcast, but not, when all is said and done, not ignoble, and so painstricken, and so pitiable!

CARD-SHARPING IN PARIS.

Paris is the home of baccarat; in Parisian soil the weed first sprouted, and has ever since rankly flourished. Where baccarat is most played, there, as a logical result, cheating is most rife. The present article is an attempt to exemplify and explain some of the least known and most peculiar modes of cheating practised in the Parisian hells.

I.

From five to six on an exquisite afternoon in early June "all Paris" swims into the ken of an idler seated *à la terrasse* of Durand's, enjoying an opal-tinted *absinthe légère*—carriages with fashionable and occasionally famous occupants going to and coming from the Avenue des Champs Elysées and the Bois; politicians, their black leather *serviette* under their arm, returning from the sitting at the Palais Bourbon across the Concorde bridge; strollers extending their patrol from the boulevard round the corner into the inviting Rue

Royale; foreigners from all countries and of all hues making their way towards the places where for the moment beats quickest the pulse of Parisian life.

Sauntering elegantly by, gloves and a stick in his right hand, his left swaying rhythmically in unison with his step, comes a well-dressed, intelligent-looking Frenchman about thirty. . . Scarcely anyone among this driving, promenading concourse knows him for aught save a member, rather more pleasing and distinguished than the rest, of the *Paris qui s'amuse*. . . I know him for a card-sharper,—a man who procures through systematic cheating at cards the means for his daily (and costly) subsistence.

. . . My interesting cheat has caught sight of me, about fifteen seconds later, perhaps, than I of him. I am gazing abstractedly at the grey-green contents of my glass, but am conscious nevertheless of the faint, thousandth part of a start which he gives on seeing me seated here. *Ticquer*, they call this movement, in French. . . . *Il a ticqué*, people say of a man who on examining his cards at baccarat cannot refrain from revealing by the slightest possible gesture that he holds an unexpectedly valuable point. *Il a ticqué*, is likewise the expression used concerning someone who shows by an irrepressible if all but imperceptible glance or quiver that he has just become aware of the presence of some other person, whom for the nonce he could wish elsewhere.

X—— is gliding by with an air of narrowly examining a "consumer" seated just three chairs beyond, when I abruptly raise my eyes. His head turns, his glance is directed straight toward me. And now a smile of perfectly admirable sincerity lights up his visage as he lifts three fingers of his left hand in salutation. The seat at my side is vacant. . . . I beckon with a certain familiar amiability,—*l'air bon enfant*, is the precise French label for it. He bows with half-sarcastic courtesy in response, and here am I demanding a second mild absinthe which a card-sharper is to place to his lips. Verily, curiosity may make us acquainted with strange drink-fellows. . . . But what does it matter, after all! This man presents to me all the interest of a psychological inquiry.

The glittering panorama of *tout Paris* unrolls itself more and more rapidly before our vision. For the instant, I am glancing at General de Gallifet in mufti recumbent on the cushions of a victoria whirling him sharply to his club near by, the "Union." Flaming forth in vivid relief against the grey tones of his travelling suit (has the General been away somewhere in the country?), his complexion recalls the hard crude redness of an Apache's. . . . Then the proud flash of the black eye, the bold curve of the aquiline nose, the soldierly leanness of the cheek —really, at sixty, a phenomenon of virility.

"*Tiens, le petit M——*," remarks my companion, drawing my attention to a phaeton driven by a gentleman who long bore in Paris, and for aught I know bears still, the somewhat operatic title of *le petit Duc*. His father was anything but *petit*. . . . And he himself began in life as the son of his father. His adventures subsequently have been as varied as peculiar. . . . The man beside me takes a sincere professional interest in this "little," or "petty," Duke.

And now, another phaeton, another M. ——, but this time, if you please, a prince. . . . An Italian prince, however; and that, as my American compatriots would phrase it, is "a horse of another colour." X—— seems no less moved than before.

"He has a brother, a Marquis," I hear him murmur, his eyes following the second glittering vehicle as it dashes along the wide expanse of the Boulevard Malesherbes just in front of us, a little to our left; a brother, *qui est encore plus fort que lui*."

Mean envy of super-eminent rivals, inability to

recognize paramount merit in his own line of endeavour, are evidently not among X——'s failings. . . . He is a card-sharper, not a latter-day *littérateur*.

". . . Yes, a vast amount of 'labour' is carried on daily, unsuspected, amongst the highest circles," X—— says in reply to some question I have just asked him. "But—on your side of the Channel . . . the case would appear to be very much the same?"

"Let us not discuss that question. If we must be 'actual,' let us exchange our views upon the subject of *poussette*."

". . . *Poussette?* Too clumsy and vulgar to be worth discussing. . . . You remember the line in the old tragedy :—

> 'Ainsi que la vertu, le crime a ses degrés . . .'

(A line, by the way, most *criminally* unpoetical). Well, the sentiment applies to matters of 'operating' at cards no less than matters of downright 'crime.' 'Degrees' there are, in the scale of 'operation.' . . . And the very lowest degree of all is that which has received the appropriately infantile title of *poussette*. Your English papers, I observe, spell the word *poucette*,—with a 'c.' Tell them, from me, that this is absurd. . . . *Poussette* comes from *pousser*, to push, and has nothing whatever to do with *pouce*, the thumb. I am foolishly fastidious, you will say, regarding such a trifle, but I confess I don't like to see the physiognomy of words, big or little, thus stupidly impaired."

"Do you remember," I remarked, "at the Cercle de la Confédération Universelle" (I confess this was not exactly the name I mentioned; but, at any rate, a name very similar) "G——, the doctor who used to come there? He would invariably, when goaded by previous losses into a state bordering on frenzy, try a *poussette* with the few louis remaining before him. And oh, the poor fellow's anguish, on one historical occasion, when, perceiving his tableau had 'eight,' he pushed his last fifty-franc counter on to the table only to hear, a second later, the banker languidly declaring 'nine'! He writhed, and grew so dangerously red, one feared lest he should have to call himself in to treat a case of apoplexy. . . . Then there was R——, who used to practise what might be styled *la poussette parlée*. 'Dix louis qui tombent,' he would observe, and if the coup won would claim them; but if the coup lost would remain scrupulously dumb. The ten louis would be claimed from him sometimes by the banker. . . . 'Oh, I meant *dix louis qui tombent* on the coup now about to take place,' would then be his reply. . . . But he generally would lose this second coup as well, and be forced, in spite of everything, to pay; raising dim reproachful eyes to heaven the while, and turning towards a neighbour in order to vent his fury and grind his teeth upon the subject of his 'luck.' . . . 'R——'s ten-louis coup?' one banker used to say to us, 'I rather delight in it myself. . . . I always feel so certain I am going to win at least twice in succession whenever I hear him announce it.'"

"But B——, Count B——," my companion responded. "You know, the son of the Russian millionaire. . . . *He* used to cultivate *poussette* in its least unpractical form. . . . Given the possession of a large initial stake (few people have sufficient strength of character to *pousseter* so long as they still have plenty of money in hand, but will generally wait before attempting it till luck has pronounced against them and they are reduced to almost the lowest ebb): given, I say, a fair amount of capital, and this *poussette* of B——'s is by no means a bad kind of 'operation.' B—— would, previous to the coup, spread out before him a large loose heap of counters or of gold. . . . If his tableau lost, his stake would be swept in bodily by the croupier's lathe, and on either side not a syllable would be uttered. . . . But, supposing the tableau won, either the croupier or the banker would ask 'Monsieur, combien à la masse?' . . . And now came the ingenious B——'s opportunity. Nonchalantly stretching out his hand, he would proceed to count over, one by one, the coins or counters composing his stake. . . . But—I need hardly add—in the palm of the hand in question would be secreted a quantity of other counters or coins, which would now invisibly find their way into the centre of the rest, and thus a coup on which, say, forty or fifty louis would stand to be lost would in the case of a win, bring in to B—— some ten or fifteen louis over and above that sum. Suppose this little feat to be performed some four or five hundred times only in the course of a baccarat year, and (through the doctrine of the equality of chances, according to which, within a certain number of turns, losing and winning coups occur in about equal proportions) the result is a comfortable income."

"Was not," I returned, "the same device long practised with distinguished success by your erstwhile friend and associate P——, at a club then situated not a hundred miles from the Place Vendôme? P—— finally was exposed.

I met him one fine evening rushing frantically upstairs into the supper-rooms of the Américain in quest of witnesses to bear his challenge the following day to his accuser. The latter refused to accept the challenge. . . . 'You may challenge me,' he said to P——, 'you may insult me, you may even try to strike me, but you shall *not* succeed in making me cross swords with you.' . . . P——'s sole remaining course was to evaporate—which he did. The *Figaro* next day published a leader on the subject from the pen of Albert Wolff; and gossip was rife upon the subject for at least forty-eight hours. One man said he knew P—— had gone to Switzerland with a lady; and, by the way, is it not astonishing how determined ladies are to go on believing in the honour of convicted cheats? Another said that P—— had 'run down' to Lake Como to sun himself throughout the winter months there in moneyed ease. Yet another would have it P—— had gone to resume his supposed former occupation of robbing stage-coaches in Spain, his native country. He at all events has not yet returned to his adopted city, Paris, which doubtless at present would receive him back with open arms. . . . He was sympathetic and had a charming tenor voice."

"Years before P—— managed to make his

way into the club, where at last he was caught red-handed," X—— went on in reply, "he had inaugurated at several 'low-down' *tripots* a mode of *poussette* hardly less ingenius and effective than his second and grander method. In front of him would be observed a hundred-franc bank-note spread out to its widest dimensions. The coup wins. P—— immediately says, 'Pardon, there are some counters here along with the note.' Croupier removes the note with the tip of his lathe, and discloses a handful of small round pieces of mother-of-pearl underneath it. But in the case of the coup's losing, P—— promptly resumes possession of the violet-tinted piece of paper, exclaiming, 'I can't let you rake in my *fétiche*, my luck-bringing hundred-franc note; I will give you counters instead.'—'The counters *and* the note, if you please, M. P——,' remarked one evening a banker a little less mole-eyed than the rest. And P—— could not but accede to the politely-formulated demand."

"Can you inform me of any other varieties of *poussette?*"

"Oh yes, there are several more ways of surreptitiously increasing one's stake after winning in addition to those we have already considered. The art, on this side of the Channel, is practised rather less crudely than on the other. . . .

One of the neatest methods of *poussetage* was that indulged in for months and months at the Cercle Trois Etoiles by a quite imposing Roumanian noble: bald, long drooping black moustache, distinguished profile and equally distinguished drawl. . . . He smoked cigarettes incessantly, played for smallish stakes but in quite the *grande manière*, and every evening would order a footman to place at his elbow a *flambeau* or candlestick, which he would raise occasionally from the table for the purpose of re-lighting his extinguished cigarette. Some keen observer—not the banker: it is my personal experience that bankers never observe: if 'straight' they are too dull to see beyond the tip of their nose, and if 'operators,' too painfully and utterly absorbed in the conduct of their 'operations'—at last became aware of the fact that the silver candlestick at the Roumanian Count's right hand was raised from the table very often after the Count's tableau had won, but never after the Count's tableau had lost. Closer inspection revealed the fact that lurking permanently beneath the foot of the candlestick, like an adder under a stone, was a large red counter for a considerable amount. The rest may be divined, and need hardly be recounted. . . . Briefly, the Roumanian Count was expelled. A few days later he was discovered comfortably seated in the reading-room's most luxurious armchair, with the Saturday supplement of the *Figaro* spread out before him. 'Sir,' sternly said a black-frock-coated member of the committee, 'are you aware your name has been struck off the list of members?'—'I understood I would not be admitted into the card-rooms,' replied the other, 'but I certainly thought I might continue to come and read the papers!!' . . .—Oh, *poussette* anecdotes in Paris are legion. . . . But why dwell upon the subject? A *pousseteur* to me is an object of contempt. . . . Too dishonest to play straight, he is not bold enough, or skilful enough, or both these things together, to 'operate' like a man and like an artist. There was Jar—, the famous Pole, in past years also a friend of . . . Princes. He cheated, was detected, and—he died. But at least *he* had always been a 'workman,' and would never have condescended to such lowness as to 'push.'"

I was moved to admire herein a fine instance of professional spirit. "Men, sir, who had they been born cobblers would all their lives have mended shoes and never made them." Such was the tone in which Goldsmith's baffled adventurer stigmatised the grovelling dulness of those whom favouritism or blind chance had placed in the highest political posts. A similarly lofty feeling of scorn it was that breathed in X——'s denunciation of the baseness of mere unadorned, "unoperative" *poussette*, as compared with the superior æsthetic beauty and nobility of "labour." Slightly to modify the French saying: "Où l'amour-*propre* va-t-il se nicher?" . . . . Introduce itself somewhere it evidently must.

II.

. . . It was the day of the *Marché aux Fleurs*, and on either side of the Madeleine church just opposite, stretched the rows of little canvas booths sheltering masses of variegated bloom. A crowd of purchasers were coming and going; along the pavement, cabs and private carriages were drawn up, into one or other of which, at every minute, some delightfully-dressed woman would clamber, her hands, like Persephone's, borne down with flowers. To the right and to the left, nearer us, on opposite sides of the broad, straight Rue Royale, the two little old-fashioned fountains, each standing sedate in its 1840 primness in the middle of its minute twin square. . . . One saw Paris, one felt it, one breathed it, and one was charmed.

X—— had turned in his seat, and, twisting thoughtfully his black moustache, was regarding me with a thin, peculiar smile. . . . "It is not for nothing that they talk of *l'œil américain*," he remarked, after a time. "I shall never forget that day at the club, when I was banking, and felt your eye was upon me. The sensation is a great deal more singular than agreeable. . . . A thread of freezing cold water trickling gently down the small of one's back. . . . I cannot conscientiously recommend you to try it. But tell me—how did you come to be an *affranchi?*"

Affranchi—literally, "a freed slave." The term, as I knew, is used by "operators" to denote one initiate in the tricks of their trade or mysteries of their art. I felt, however, I could not justly lay claim to the honours of the title, and I intimated as much to my companion.

"But at all events you are *voyant*—a 'seer'—that much you cannot possibly deny?"

Voyant appeared to me complimentary, without being of necessity degrading. To this fact of my simply "seeing," I concluded, therefore, I might safely own.

"And how, may I inquire, did you first find yourself gifted with 'vision'?" . . . Thus, again, X——, politely persistent.

"H—m—m . . . .Rather a long story perhaps,

. . . In one word, I suppose it was because, having eyes, I used them. I was taken to my first club about fifteen years ago (I was not of age at the time, but the people of the place asked no particularly indiscreet questions) by a *racoleur* [tout or 'bonnet'] who had scraped acquaintance with me at a café. The second day of my 'membership' I was punting at the table. . . . Enormous banks throughout the night; the croupier incessantly kept busy sorting out counters and erecting them in separate piles, according to order of value, in front of him; and the *cagnotte* [the drawer into which the croupier lets fall, through a slot in the baccarat-table within easy reach of his hand, the percentage levied upon the sum bid for each 'bank' or deal], what with new banks in rapid succession and the frequent renewal of the same bank, getting hourly fuller and fuller. 'Je ne passe jamais deux fois,' a man exclaimed as he indignantly threw up his cards after drawing a seven to a tray. 'En voilà une qui passe tout le temps,' replied his neighbour, pointing towards the insatiable slot, in which the croupier at that very moment was insinuating three red twenty-franc counters, one on the heels of the other. The observation seemed to me highly significant, as well as sensible.—Years passed, during which the clubs saw me all too often. To go to one of them of course meant going to ——"

"But it really is too kind of you," X—— interrupted, "to bestow the name of 'clubs' on these places where you had the dishonour of making my acquaintance."

"True. But seeing that there are in Paris only some half-dozen clubs properly so-called, and about ten times as many more which are simply hells of the rankest description, and yet that each and all of these places apply to themselves the same generic title, some excuse may be found for my inaccurate expression. Let us say *tripot*, if you like, or even *claquedents* [a word of unknown etymology signifying the lowest form of hell], and *n'en parlons plus*. . . . What the attractions of the *tripots* were I assuredly needn't remind you. Perchance in ante-professional days, you were not insensible to the same yourself? To pay five francs or, more generally speaking, nothing—once the people of the house had set you down as what they term an *élément sérieux* there was no such thing as getting them to give you a bill—for a dinner worth to them twelve or fifteen francs, and to you, perhaps, nearer five-and-twenty, eaten in company with some of the drollest beings extant on the *pavé de Paris*, was unquestionably a feature. . . . Then the soirées' and the 'fêtes. . . .' Personally I didn't find these quite so entertaining; but that probably is because I have always shrunk with horror from anything like amateur, or at least, impromptu, concerts or theatricals. Other 'members' were, I daresay, less ungratefully disposed towards a bountiful 'administration' that monthly or even weekly would provide for their entertainment music by some of the best singers of the day and interludes by celebrated actresses and actors upon the ten-foot-square stage contrived at the far end of the *salle-à-manger*, where rows of *fauteuils* and of red-plush-covered chairs would be placed by way of constituting an auditorium. Then again, the fancy dress and other balls! . . . Oh, those balls, and the lady guests invited thereunto! . . . Venus, coming as nearly as she dared in the same costume that secured to her the apple, to dazzle, amid the lofty halls of Plutus, every banking as well as punting eye. . . . Pre-eminently Parisian, was it not?"

X—— laughed, and I paused, my mind oppressed with the luxuriance of these memories of my *claquedents* years.

"You remember those banks of quadruple power," I continued, after a reinvigorating sip at my largely tempered absinthe, "that used to follow upon the marvellous 'soirées'? . . . .

Banks welcome to players and 'directors' alike. . . . The scene on those nights of high-pressure dealing at the fashionable Paris *cercles*—never, so long as I live, shall I forget it. . . . The banker, croupier, and a dozen punters occupying seats at the oval table; thirty or forty more people standing crowded together behind; the general breathless silence preceding every important coup, and the hubbub of contradictory comment immediately following. . . . The gestures, the exclamations, the grimaces. . . . Such costumes, such countenances, such types . . . . You would have thought the entire world was here represented by the pick of its 'delicate monsters,' as Shakespeare has it in *The Tempest.* Englishmen stupidly stiff; Russians and Poles with waxed moustaches and names ending in 'off' and 'sky;' Roumanians, all eyes, beard, and fingers ever writhing like the feelers of the octopus; Yankees, noted for the harrowing harshness of their tones in declaring (far too frequently) the point of 'weet;' citron-tinted and bediamonded Diazes, Pedros, and Lopezes; Germans, generally with bushy beards, and who always were Swiss, Danes, or Swedes, unless natives of Alsace-Lorraine; Levantines, speaking equally badly every language under the sun; Hebrews hailing from the four quarters of the universe;

Frenchmen from every province in France, and especially from the Meridional departments. . . . Once at a *tripot* I beheld a Chinaman in national costume of gown, pigtail, and cap surmounted by a tiny glass button; whilst blacks of every degree of blackness were anything but uncommon. Now imagine this conglomerate mass swaying, seething, and speaking, or rather squeaking, squalling, gabbling, babbling, squabbling, and bawling in a monstrously over-heated and over-lighted room, for hours and hours at a stretch; eye and ear being reminded of nothing so much as a sort of very disorderly human Noah's Ark. There are some delightful passages in Smollett (Smollett, an English novelist of the last century, with whom you, my dear X——, are indubitably unacquainted) that might have been written after passing a night at any one of twenty or thirty houses within a half-mile radius of the Opera and the Vaudeville Theatre. Why has no modern French writer given us an adequate *étude de tripot?*—For, of course, I do not apply the title of writers to that pair of persons calling themselves respectively Ricouard and Vast, who produced a publication called *Le Tripot*, and are now, very properly, both dead, nor to an excellent tradesman of my acquaintance, Hector Malot by name, who once prepared for sale a certain article of commerce labelled *Baccara*—without the "t". Why hasn't Daudet, for example . . ."

"Neither Daudet nor any one else has done it, for the simple but sufficient reason that it cannot be done. . . . A Parisian baccarat-room in full ebullition—a hundred different things leaping at you, as it were, all at once—fifty men, each with his peculiar individuality, his idiosyncrasy or *tic*, and each displaying this *tic* at one and the same moment; in the observer's eye and mind, a sort of rapidly-shifting glitter, a *papillottement* as of twenty giant kaleidoscopes simultaneously revolving. . . . How to put such things on paper, unless the pen is used as Delacroix wanted draughtsmen to use the pencil, when he said they should be able to sketch a man during the time he was falling from a fifth-storey window to the ground? No; you writers should reflect oftener upon the limitations of your art. But . . . *Pardon* . . . you were telling me how you came to be a 'seer.'"

Decidedly, he held to it. . . . He had made up his mind to learn the precise extent of my ignorance or knowledge. I, for my part, determined that at all events he should elicit no more from me than I from him.

"It was *chemin de fer* (a form of the game of

baccarat in which each player deals in turn, until his hand loses, instead of the cards being dealt from beginning to end by a single banker opposed to the punters *en masse*), as I imagine, that first put me on the track; first directed me, I should say, towards the regions of 'philosophic' wisdom. For I believe you use the old term, 'Greek,' no longer,—'philosophers' is how you style yourselves at present?"

"My dear sir, you are behind the time. . . . There are no more Greeks, no more philosophers, only Bedouins."

"Bedouins?"

"Of course you perceive the allusion. . . . The Arab chieftain, his long gun slung upon his shoulder, scouring the plains upon the back of his long-tailed steed, and pouncing, hawk-like, upon his prey; if pursued, rapidly disappearing amid the trackless expanse of the desert.—But you were saying . . . *Chemin de fer?*"

"*Chemin de fer*, as you know, used to be introduced at the clubs in the wee sma' hours (or, rather, not small hours, but hours quickly lengthening on their way towards high noon) when the last of the evening's bankers had dealt his last, long, lingering deal. . . . Plenty of money was still to be found among the phalanx of the punters, but no one punter with either courage or funds sufficient to venture a bank in his turn. . . . Then the nine packs (*chemin de fer*, in Paris clubs, is generally played with nine packs shuffled together) would be introduced, a certain undercurrent of sprightliness would appear to set in amongst a special group, and, singularly enough, to the different members of that group would invariably go the bulk of the money subsequently lost and won. I would sit—I blush now to declare it—for hours observing the course of the play; but could never detect anything absolutely or actively incorrect. Yet that some latent or passive kind of 'operation' was going forward, I found it impossible to doubt. . . . I——"

Here I was abruptly interrupted.

"Have you ever heard," X—— asked me, "of what is called *la séquence?*"

I felt now that enlightenment was at hand, concerning what I had always deemed a most curious and mysterious problem.

"On an average in a *chemin de fer* deal with nine packs," my instructor presently began, "there will occur between ninety and one hundred coups. *La séquence* is a method of arrangement according to which each one of these coups, losing or winning, is unmistakably known before hand to persons possessing the 'key' or clue. . . .

The thing is perpetrated as follows. Four hundred and sixty-eight cards, composing the prescribed nine packs, have previously been placed card by card in a certain order, so calculated that the last card of each coup played will indicate the result of the coup to follow. Only a very slight effort of memory is required in order to recall what the particular cards are that mean 'the next coup wins,' or 'the next coup loses,' as the case may be. A variety of *séquences* are known and daily put in use. All are similarly simple, all similarly unerring."

"—Highly interesting," I interjected. "But tell me—is there never any difficulty in becoming cognizant of that valuable and obliging 'last card'? I don't exactly perceive——"

"No difficulty whatsoever. . . . How could there be? We will suppose you are holding the cards. . . . You deal a card to your opponent, one to yourself, one to opponent again and one again to yourself, this latter being the last of the hand. Consequently you will keep it a little apart, so as not to confound it with its companion card, combining with it to constitute your point. Two more cards, however, according to the rules of the game, may be dealt on the coup if desired: one to your opponent, and one to yourself, or, perhaps, only one to your opponent. In this latter case—that of being called on to deal one or two cards additional on a coup – I needn't point out to you how great is the facility for gaining a knowledge of the last card. For these supplementary cards, as you know, are dealt separately, and face upwards."

. . . "At present," I replied, "it is all quite clear to me. And at length I cease to wonder at the singularly bad luck of some of the players at the games of *chemin de fer* I was wont to take part in, and the singularly good luck of certain others. Playing *chemin de fer* with a 'sequence' is much what backing horses would be, if the backer had some occult means of foreseeing the exact order in which every runner was destined to pass the post. It is a species of terrific chain, this sequence of yours, unfolding itself pitilessly link after link; or else a kind of Juggernaut, nine packs long, with a victim flattened out at every revolution of the wheel. One point only remains to be explained. . . . It strikes me that even the slightest amount of shuffling would do away with the order of your sequence? . . . And isn't the croupier supposed to shuffle the whole nine packs up together the moment they are placed upon the table?"

"Is it possible that you—you—do not know how easily experts can simulate a shuffle? . . .

The nine packs are set before the croupier. He rapidly plays upon them with his fingers (*jouer de l'accordéon* is the name this operation goes by); the cards move, his fingers move, but meanwhile not a single piece of pasteboard has changed its position. Only that style of shuffling termed *la salade,* and which consists in spreading the whole of the cards out before one on the table, and as it were churning or kneading them up together, is effectual in extinguishing a *séquence.*"

"The information," I replied, "has its value. . . . The sole weapon, as I gather, to be opposed against the horrors of *la séquence* is this admirable and invaluable *salade.* To employ an extravagant simile, which Hugo would not have hesitated to adopt: *la salade* is the mongoose, to be pitted against *la séquence* cobra. . . . Now seeing that, at a *tripot,* each particular *ponte* is entitled to insist upon the cards being radically "beaten," as the French term goes, it would be amusing, I think, as well as hygienic, to sternly call for *la salade,* and then observe the expression on the countenances of certain players."

"Yes, yes," my interlocutor rejoined, "but pray refrain from making any such experiment if you see *me* seated at the table."

. . . "Decidedly, the more I think of it, the more clearly I perceive this *séquence* to be about the most appalling method of butchery (cheating is too delicate a word) which I ever yet have heard of. By the side of all other modes of 'operation,' it is the Gatling gun compared to the horse-pistol or the blunderbuss."

Thus I remarked, after a pause which X—— and myself had been devoting to our respective meditations. He, probably speculating as to whether, having so far completed my initiation, he might not be able to gain me over as a "philosophic" recruit. . . . And I reflecting, without much amazement after all (for this pastime we denominate Life, is it not made up of an infinitude of results no less ironically absurd?), to what uses my present companion's qualities and gifts of manner and mind, intelligence, amenity, distinction, were being devoted. . . .

"Other modes of 'operation' say you? Other modes of 'operation' at *chemin de fer?* Am I to understand that you are acquainted with any such?" asks X——, not perhaps without a touch of amiable satire.

. . . It is my turn now to convince him that my powers of "vision" are less restricted than he imagines.

"Oh, yes; I fancy I have had occasion to observe a number of them before to-day."

". . . As, for example?" . . .

"—Coal-black hair, snaky moustache, lemon-coloured complexion, dark eyes that seemed to snap: a Meridional, seated early one morning at the baccarat table; one morning in budding spring, keen threads of reproachful daylight forcing their brightness into the gas-lit sweltering room through the crevices in the tall closed shutters and hinting irksomely at a fresh, clean, sun-lit world without. . . . During the course of a game at *chemin de fer*, which I cannot now doubt to have been of a nature entirely 'sequential,' the hand reached my Meridional, whose eyes hereupon fell to snapping faster and harder than ever. 'Il y a cinq louis à la main,' he proclaimed, with the most fearful Toulouse twang I have ever yet heard—out of Toulouse. Instantly one of the players 'in the swim' jumped, like a pike at a spoon, at the unknown player's bet. 'Pardon,' continued the Meridional, 'fifty instead of five!' 'All right!' returned the other, a shade more greedily than before. The cards are dealt, and—'Nine!' declares the Meridional.—Fierce amazement on the part of his opponent, who glares, with various sentiments contending for (and yet debarred from) expression, at his own point, then at his adversary's, then at the fifty louis as they are passed at the point of the croupier's lathe to swell the heap of the amiably smiling Meridional; and then finally at the faces of several people at the table, which faces meanwhile had become very nearly as long as the glarer's. My conclusion concerning this incident was arrived at very promptly."

"And it was?" . . . X—— asked, his eye fixed rather curiously upon me.

". . . Simply that the Meridional, believing for reasons of his own that the coup, as it reached him, was certain to be a losing one, first ingeniously succeeded, on the strength of this certitude in the minds of the 'operators' present, to provoke a good large wager; and thereupon, calmly and comfortably proceeded to '*take the second.*'"

A very minor *coup de théâtre* this last little speech of mine, yet X—— started visibly as he heard the last three words. . . . And I was somewhat gratified. . . . .

"What do you know about *taking the second?*" he asked, a thought more abruptly than was his wont.

"I know—all one need know, without going the lengths of doing the thing oneself. Besides, X——, you forget. . . First day at the club. . .

Thread of ice-cold water trickling down the small of the back. . . . You were speaking about it yourself, not twenty minutes ago."

This time, actually though slightly, my companion blushed. . .

"And of course . . ." I went on blandly, with an ample, expressive, outward wave of the hand; "of course you will perceive that by this 'taking' or 'slipping' of the 'second,' my lemon-hued Meridional exactly *reversed* the expected result of his coup. Conjecturing that the first and third cards of the hand, due legitimately to his adversary, were known beforehand to be winning ones, whilst the second and fourth cards, reverting to himself, were bound undoubtedly to lose, he simply, by the performance of that little sleight-of-hand act of 'slipping,' which *some* people, my dear Sir, have brought to such an exquisite pitch of perfection, dealt cards second and fourth to his opponent, holding back meanwhile cards first and third for himself. . . A neat and delicate device, but, I should say, not likely to be effected very often."

III.

. . . A long silence ensued, and then: —"Any further revelations for my benefit?" X—— inquired, drawing a handkerchief from his pocket and flicking a few stray grains of dust from the surface of an ornate, pointed, patent-leather shoe. "Any further startling data on the subject of 'operations' in general? Decidedly, you are a well of science. . . ."

"— Oh, I will not overwhelm you with the weight of my special knowledge. . . . I will only say that I have become acquainted, wholly and solely through the effect of oft-renewed and attentive observation and of careful and discreet inquiry in more directions than one, with the following typical methods of 'besting' either dealer or punters, as the case may be, at 'the bank' or at *chemin de fer*. When I shall have completed my enumeration, you will see that *la séquence*, which you have to-day so lucidly explained, was perhaps the one form of 'operatîon' with which I was not previously acquainted —in theory only, let me entreat you to believe."

X—— gazed at me without a word, but with a highly sympathetic smile, and raised, in mock courtesy, his impeccably "correct," not too vulgarly glossy hat.

"First, then, there is the *neuf de campagne* or *coup de la Minerve*. . . . This consists in simply 'springing' on the dealer a nine prepared beforehand, and secreted somewhere about the person.

Why called 'Minerve' I cannot imagine, unless because, like Minerva from the brain of Jove, it starts full-fledged into existence from the breast of the 'operator's' coat or dim recesses of his sleeve. Secondly, the *mirior*, a device by which the 'operator,' to gain the necessary knowledge of the cards with which he is playing, holds them slightly apart so that a keen-eyed confederate, called the 'telegraphist,' can 'signal' him which is the most useful to be 'taken.' . . . Then the *placard* or *emplâtre*, the 'plaster' bodily 'stuck on' to the top of the pack: meaning, obviously, the introduction into the game of a certain number of cards either subtracted from those in use at the time on the table, or else of extraneous derivation, but in each case so prepared as to furnish forth a certain number of assured winning coups. . . . Then the bold, dangerous, but admirably effective *coup de la ceinture*, as effective with regard to 'banking' as *la séquence*, which it somewhat resembles, is with regard to *chemin de fer*. . . . *La ceinture*, as *you* well know, is the substitution of a complete banking deal at one fell swoop. The banker takes in hand the three packs of cards placed before him to be shuffled. In a specially adapted belt around his waist three other packs lie in waiting. And a moment later —hey presto! *ni vu ni connu*—the three packs in the waistband and the three packs upon the table have changed positions, with immediate subsequent results not very difficult to imagine. This coup, as I have been informed, flourishes more particularly in large watering places and the capitals of foreign countries.—Finally there is the art of marking cards, so that their value may be recognised from the mere covert inspection of their backs. If desired to be effected without the knowledge or complicity of the croupier or proprietors of the club (which, for certain pecuniary reasons is not always to be obtained), 'marking' becomes a matter somewhat awkward to accomplish. The problem was once ingeniously solved by a gentleman who wore spectacles with darkened glasses, and day after day dealt banks of a simply murderous description. The people of the house felt convinced it was a case of 'operation.' The croupier, indeed, vowed he could hear from where he sat the hissing of the cards as they were slipped, though, of course, nothing was visible to the naked eye. 'Hissing' (as who, my dear X——, should know better than yourself?) is the great, almost insurmountable difficulty an 'operator' has to contend against. They tell a story, indeed, of some 'laborious' person from Bordeaux, who in a moment of expansion declared that for three years he practised in a room, darkened, for the better concentration of his hearing, until—'Enfin, j'ai remercié le bon Dieu! Je ne m'entendais plus. . . . The sound of my slipping was at last inaudible to myself!'—he fervently exclaimed, and ever after 'slipped' but 'hissed' no more. . . . To revert, however, to my man with blackened goggles: after each deal the backs and faces of the cards would be microscopically examined, but . . . nothing, nothing, nothing! The good people of the house were in despair. . . . Finally, a second wearer of smoked glasses was observed to take his stand behind the banker. . . . A member of the 'committee' this person; and at the second coup he rushed out, beckoning all his associates to follow him. 'Sacré nom d'un chien!' he cried as soon as the party were assembled in a little out-of-the-way room. 'Every blessed one of those cards is marked on the back with phosphorous! He has phosphorous on the tips of his fingers!!!'—The lucky banker perhaps continued to be lucky elsewhere; but from that day forth punters who had been writhing beneath his scourge at the Cercle des Arts Héraldiques knew him no more.—And now let me consider. . . . Ah, yes, one more well-known method of 'operation.' . . . The 'putting up' by the dealer of two, three, or more coups, according to his capacity, in connection with the opening of a bank. . . . Dealer simulates a shuffle (that very feat of whose existence you were kind enough to apprise me about a quarter of an hour ago), and the trick is done. Two, three or more 'naturals' occur, and the banker is at liberty to abandon his bank if he wishes, and thus to secure to himself his gains, beyond the possibility of loss. He will doubtless, however, continue to 'play' ('playing,' in contradistinction from 'working') and in that case, encountering the well-known luck of the 'Bedouin,' will infallibly and invariably lose back all he had won and more. '*Coups montés*' is, by-the-bye, the professional name applied to this final device I have mentioned.—With this, I think, I have given you a fair idea of how much or how little is 'known' to me. I might indeed go on to remind you of the 'palming' or 'crushing' of counters from off the table by the croupier, meaning their systematic though naturally invisible conveyance into the ever-gaping pocket at his side, containing usually sand or sawdust to deaden the sound of the counters as they fall. Strange tales might be told of deeds of 'écrasage' and 'bourrage' accomplished on such a scale in Paris clubs that in the course of a few months, at a place close behind the Opera, a sum of three hundred thousand francs was 'lifted' or 'gathered' by a single croupier, officiating in the midst of an exceedingly heavy game where, naturally, both dealers and punters lost. All this might now be treated of, and likewise the *mangeurs* or blackmailers, who live in luxury by simply ransoming 'operating' philosophers on the one hand, and counter-crushing croupiers on the other, all round with masterly impartiality. . . . But these things are not art, they are not 'operation,' they are merely vulgar robbery. . . . And our discourse is of higher things."

"You are somewhat hard . . ." X—— answered, as he rose to go.

M. MAURICE BARRÈS.

Ample vesture, and so meagre a frame beneath; sleek body, with a soul starveling as well as corrupt—is not that the main impression conveyed by much of the most noticeable French literature of the hour, literature not only lost to the sense of virtue, but hardly even alive to the full, fell power of passion or vice; base torpidly, wicked frigidly, sinful labouriously with a view to the acquisition of *gros sous* thereby; latter-day Gautiers and Baudelaires distilling strange filth in the columns of boulevard prints, lineal descendants of Mérimée and Flaubert chiefly devoting their skill to the analysis of abomination; Cellinis, in a word, who are for ever carving obscenities, and that, too, less for love of the thing than on account of the material advantages of the trade.

These are doubtless extreme considerations, applying to particular (albeit all too typical) cases, and which none will be inclined to take as covering the entire field of contemporary French letters. Who can deny, however, that this poverty, this pettiness, indeed almost vileness of inward life, as contrasting with a well-nigh unprecedented degree of exterior refinement and perfection, pervades some of the highest as well as lowest writing of the day in France, from M. Renan to M. Mendès, and constitutes its chief characteristic? The art, admirable and exquisite; the artist, so often, very nearly the reverse . . .

With M. Maurice Barrès, nearly alone amid such a number of soulless artists or else of inartistic "honest" writers, art and feeling go hand in hand. For this sole reason, if for none other, the author of *Sous l'Œil des Barbares*, *Un Homme Libre* and *Le Jardin de Bérénice* would deserve the honours of a formal introduction to the English public.

I.

. . . Uncertain, brooding, refined—physically and morally delicate, in both the more and the less favourable sense of that term; possessing, or rather possessed by, sympathies quick, ardent and eager, susceptibilities all but overpowering, yet held in check by the proud timidity peculiar to certain natures in which the moral elements so far outweigh the material: such, at twenty, was M. Barrès, typical young Frenchman of the finest, the so-much-too-fine type, when, after the usual French collegiate education, he came up from his native province, Lorraine, to Paris as the intellectual centre of France, and to the "Latin Quarter" as the intellectual centre of Paris.

"The usual French collegiate education." . . . All that is implied by this phrase, those alone who have undergone the experience will comprehend. M. Barrès would, I am convinced, share the sentiments to which Baudelaire, himself a victim, gave voice in his melancholy lines:—

> "Nous traînions tristement nos ennuis, accroupis
> Et voûtés sous le ciel carré des solitudes
> Où l'enfant boît, dix ans, l'âpre lait des études."

Maurice Barrès, like the author of the *Fleurs du Mal*, knew well those "wastes," walled-in so frowningly on every side, with, overhead, only that "square" patch of sky. . . In a characteristically quaint remark at the opening of the first chapter of *Sous l'Œil des Barbares*, some of the consequences of French collegiate life are thus denoted:—

"Insufficient nourishment made his blood poor; in consequence he grew timid, and the agitation of his manner, due to a mixture of pride and uneasiness, produced generally an unfavourable impression."

The Latin Quarter existence entered upon some eight or ten years ago by this "timidly agitated" youth no doubt presented the customary Latin Quarter features: empty lounging evenings in the hall and gardens of the Bullier ball; long and excessively multiloquent sittings at first one and then another of a dozen or score of *brasseries littéraires* and *brasseries à femmes*, the "Vachette," the "d'Harcourt," the "Furet," the "Soufflot," or the "Cigarette"; nocturnal symposia and agapæ in the rooms (rent anywhere from five-and-twenty to sixty or seventy francs a month) of friends of congenial literary tendencies and tastes.

Every young man of letters with anything in him feels impelled to plunge into depths of admiration for certain other men of letters, his immediate seniors and predecessors. Verlaine, Mallarmé, Bourget, were the gods of M. Barrès' early adoration. Truly a highly comprehensible choice. . . For the first-named among these three is a poet great even as the greatest, and pitiful and terrible beyond compare; the second, M.

Mallarmé, an interesting and original artist in words; third, M. Bourget, the most generally distinguished writer of the 1870 generation, his talent from year to year expanding and being destined—founded as it is upon the sincerest affection for and widest knowledge of true letters—indefinitely to expand in the future. To the feet of M. Bourget, in particular, did Maurice Barrès bring the tribute of his juvenile devotion. And here I think it interesting to adduce a passage from M. Barrès' more recent prose, both as conveying some sense of his peculiar literary "note," and as bearing possibly a reference to certain points of his history and career:—

"At eighteen I had a disdainful, timid revolted mind. I met a sceptic, of infinitively soft and caressing manners; but who in reality suffered no one to get near him.

"O friend, whose name I withhold, in consideration for your delicacy, I was awkward and confused; thus it was perhaps that you did not fully understand how well I understood you; perhaps you did not completely apprehend my delight at the abundance of your intellectual riches. You made me feel pain when you showed so little desire to embellish the young life which was hanging upon your words: draped in the desire to please as in a flowing garment, your chief concern was to appear ingenious in your own eyes. . . . . You captivated my soul, without even deigning to become aware of its graces; and you towed it along in your wake, from time to time casting it the sop of some flattering remark devoid of application."

Are they not redolent, these lines—whose charm, unfortunately but unavoidably, to so great an extent evaporates through the process of translation—with a grace at once ingenious and ingenuous? What juster, subtler shades of expression could be employed to mark the delicate melancholy of a too delicate soul on discovering that the gifts, attractions, faculties, powers of some nature more robust, but also less exquisitely rare, which has elicited its admiring homage, excited its intellectual love, are not presided over by a delicacy quite so extreme and supreme as its own? It would fain, in the ardour of its affection, impart to the other the one lacking, crowning grace of its own superior distinction, and it sighs to feel that this cannot be.

The literary apprenticeship served by M. Barrès was of a character less material than moral; by which I mean that prior to producing his first notable work he had talked, read, and thought much more than he had actually written. A few articles in "independent" and "decadent" Latin Quarter Journals and reviews; a little short-lived literary monthly, edited and compiled entirely by him under the title of *Les Taches d'Encre;* a slender characteristic monograph, headed *Sensations de Paris—le Quartier*

Latin, in which M. Barrès' peculiar vein of sentiment so suggestive of the union of an old head with a young heart veils itself delicately beneath a surface-glitter of felicities: this was about the extent of M. Barrès' literary output up to the time of his approving himself undoubtedly a *littérateur* with his striking *Sous l'Œil des Barbares*. It now became apparent that his fallow years had not been without their subterraneous formative influences upon his character and talent. Gautier, writing of Baudelaire's early Parisian existence, characterised it as a period of *flânerie féconde;* and the same expression might be applied to the Latin Quarter novitiate of M. Barrès, from which we find him, after some four or five years, emerging as an admired and applauded author—for *Sous l'Œil des Barbares* won the young writer immediate literary recognition. Is he not happy, by the bye, the artist and thinker whose pecuniary circumstances admit of his indulging in that "fruitful *far niente*" of Gautier's, which the unfortunate "Théo" himself was never permitted to enjoy? Well it was for M. Barrès and his readers that no material considerations interfered to prevent his bringing forth from the first, no matter at what cost of time and of labour, the best that was in him! He had not to undergo that process known as "writing for one's bread," which upon certain rough-and-ready temperaments perhaps may exercise beneficial effects, but can only mean distortion and abortion for talents of a nature more difficult, more delicate, and therefore more original and rare. He had no need to besiege with offers of and essays at "collaboration" these sworn enemies (barring some exceptions, how few!) of whatsoever is new, searching, and sincere, the editors of daily, weekly, and other publications. Not his was the horrible task of having to throw into some sort of extemporaneous form articles on various subjects and in various styles, to which a certain amount of maturing, could it only have been bestowed, would have imparted the absent qualities of tone, significance, and worth. He, in a word, was under no obligation of forcing from his brain products which that brain was never designed to bear. Sufficiently well-to-do, he was able to write only what he liked how he liked; and *O si sic omnes!* must be, in this regard, the aspiration of every other writer.

—"Voici," says M. Barrès in the preface to his *Barbares*, "une courte monographie réaliste." A "realistic" monograph; the epithet is here very properly employed, for what other realities so real as the inner realities of an autobiographer's mind? And the author adds, with perfect truth and fine precision, "That which we call reality is for each one of us a different thing, reality being only the sum of a person's ways of seeing, feeling, and thinking." His own reality it is which he proposes to body forth in his book, and not a reflection of the reality of somebody else. *Sous l'Œil des Barbares* is, in consequence, necessarily and entirely a production of the "personal" order.

"*Whilst attending carefully to the sequence of the thoughts and the graces of the vocabulary*, I have striven, above all, exactly to reproduce those images of the universe which I found superposed within my conscience. Herein will be found some account of the 'prentice years of a 'me'—soul or spirit." In those few words is exposed the whole tenour of M. Barrès' writings. If I have emphasized one of the clauses, this is because, in the suggestion thereby afforded of a highly intellectual mind disdaining to cover over or palliate the triviality, natural and inevitable, of its own more mechanical processes, but rather, since it cannot possibly evade them, bringing them humourously and carelessly to light, the passage in question is very characteristic of its author. The pseudo-artist and pseudo-philosopher — as, let us say, for a specially shocking instance, Bulwer Lytton—thinks to dignify the essential pettiness of what might be termed the stage machinery of his art by casting around it flimsy veils of flaunting gauze. The true philosopher and artist, as M. Barrès, is led, through one of the strongest impulses of his nature, to eschew all affectation of nobility in things not of themselves noble. Indispensable is this tendency, among others, to the existence of anything like true realism; of anything like the spirit informing such a production as *John Inglesant*, for example, and rendering it more real than any of the text-books of the so-called self-styled "realistic" school.—Chance brings beneath my pen the title of perhaps the finest moral study written in the English tongue during the past generation. Let me improve the opportunity by stating that throughout M. Barrès' works there breathes a tone of mingled contemplation, aspiration, and sadness, by no means dissimilar from that distinguishing Mr. Shorthouse's exquisite psychological romance. Another English writer whom this young French writer recalls is Sterne, through his natural inclination to be brilliantly and charmingly artificial, through the acuity of sensibilities verging sometimes on perversity, and through that rare admixture of an invincible innate egotism (employing the word in its least unfavourable acceptation) with an eager, constant, sincere desire for the fondness of others at whatever cost of ingenuity, endeavour, and exertion. To live and feel at once so much for oneself and so much for one's fellows is a privilege—painful privilege!—accorded to but few in a world where the rankest savagery of instinct, thinly disguising itself beneath a crust of what we flatteringly style "civilization" is the *primum mobile* of the vast majority of beings.

The disgusted aversion of a young, infinitely sensitive and clairvoyant nature from this general savagery of human-kind is the theme of *Sous l'Œil des Barbares.*—How, in the midst of so much that is distracting, shall this nature achieve the inner harmony of self? Such is the problem studied in a hundred different ways and under a hundred different phases by M. Barrès. "An inquiry into the art and science of self-culture" might be the best label for the whole trilogy, *Sous l'Œil des Barbares, Un Homme Libre*, and *Le Jardin de Bérénice*, to which the *Barbares* serves as introduction. Needless to add that on the strength of such a plan and design every petty scribbler for "Parisian" sheets, every *bel esprit* of "Parisian" drawing-rooms, every "sarcast," to borrow Mr. Gladstone's recent neologism, of "Parisian" coteries in the Montmartre and Latin Quarter pothouses, for some years past has facilely and frequently "scored" by representing the new psychologist as having deliberately exceeded all previous bounds of literary affectation and conceit. But M. Barrès has doubtless ere now discovered that opposition from certain quarters is more genuinely flattering and encouraging than any amount of sympathy and approbation encountered elsewhere.

Sous l'Œil des Barbares, whilst gaining much from its ingenuity and originality of presentment, on the other hand loses not a little from the occasional obscurity and tortuousness of its diction. Tortuousness in a young writer is often a promising fault—giving unmistakable token of earnestness and sincerity of feeling, struggling painfully, for both the writer and the reader, to express themselves through the as yet unsurmounted difficulties of a medium so much less pliable than mere thought. Nothing easier than to write nothings with freedom, fluency, and finish: *vide* the columns of the English daily and weekly literary press. The operation of amalgamating a little of one's "grey matter" with one's prose is less unlaboriously accomplished. M. Barrès, however, soon gained greater deftness at the making of this mixture than appeared in certain portions of his earliest book.

"Départ Inquiet"—"Tendresse"—"Désintéressement"—"Paris à Vingt Ans"—"Dandysme"—"Extase"—"Affaissement" and, finally, "Oraison," the respective titles of the chapters of *Sous l'Œil des Barbares*, suggest sufficiently that in each of these divisions is expressed or at all events adumbrated some new and different state of interior being on the part of the hero and writer. And to each chapter is prefixed a little commentary or "concordance," marking in a few delicately ironical phrases how the psychologist's intellect from first to last sat apart, viewing with a smile like that Da Vinci gave to all his faces, the varied adventures and emotions of the struggling, chafing, questioning soul, its mate. This intellect, this all-perceptive, essentially emotionless, ever wary and watchful intellect, bound up together with this soul so eternally eager and purturbed—how strange and particular a combination, presented by so many of the rarest and finest natures! Genius, for all its continual simulacrum of feeling, yet never does feel quite spontaneously and directly, and perhaps in a sense may be said never to feel at all. Thus we find M. Barrès giving expression to a sentiment denounced by some excellent critic as an instance of monstrous callousness of nature: "I was never really touched by exterior beauty. The finest spectacles to me are nothing more than psychological suggestions." Amiel, likewise, who was not a genius, but at any rate a most subtle and acute thinker, wrote: "A landscape is a state of the soul." And Milton and Wordsworth, and Shakespeare and Shelley, had they been narrowly sounded on the point, would, one fancies, have had to confess that with them the case was the same. Genius is, and cannot but be, complexity; and underlying, like an Undine at the bottom of a brawling brook, all the surface-agitations to which complexity gives rise, is a certain weird lack of genuine sensibility, which in the history of genius throughout the ages again and again has been seen coming to the top and there revealing itself with various disconcerting results.

From the discrepancies of human affection, the disturbances of carnal passion, the weariness and emptiness of erudition and the acridness of worldly knowledge, which in divers allegorical forms are exemplified in the opening pages of *Sous l'Œil des Barbares*, the young seeker after peace turns away to an enthusiastic contemplation of beauty, intelligence, and virtue in the legendary past. Hypatia, the martyred priestess of Alexandria, becomes for a while his idol. In a dithyramb of sustained elevation of feeling and purely classic nobility of form, he celebrates the final phases of her brief existence and brings vividly into relief the symbolic horrors of her death. I will not seek to make any quotations from this minute masterpiece, finished and perfect within itself. It is a flawless statuette, and since I cannot think to show it entire, I shall refrain at least from hacking away a finger or a toe.

The Parisian experiences of the hero of *Sous l'Œil des Barbares*, next in order in the book, offer a more favourable field for citation.

"At Paris he did not find the exceptional personalities he had dreamt of, and on account of whom he had been despising himself for years." As a small specimen of M. Barrès' powers of satire—self-satire, too, which is more—that phrase may be left to the consideration of any discriminative reader. Again, this characterisation of the peculiar "agreeableness" of Parisian life: "As to the amiable pleasure one encounters there at every turn in the street or the conversation" [in my desperate desire to preserve some remnants of M. Barrès' verbal *esprit*, I perceive I am outraging the genius of the English tongue], "he deemed that somewhat more of this would be required in order to render it satisfying." M. Barrès abounds in epigrammatic quips of this description, as pleasing, precise, polished, pungent in the original as they appear flat, strained and void when rendered in any foreign medium. His wit (and as George Eliot, who possessed so little of the quality, remarked justly: Wit is an exquisite product of high powers") is of an order connecting him less with the vulgar *fin de siècle* spirit of *blague* than with the foremost French traditions. Larochefoucauld, Labruyère, Chamfort, would not blush to own M. Barrès for a successor.

But this young man's years of inward contention and unrest amid the ever-shifting Parisian world, himself, at soul, shifting the most incessantly of all, have not been made by him a subject for the exercise of his *esprit* alone. Epigram is but the salt, the Attic salt, wherewith he flavours the *ensemble* of his anxious metaphysical searchings, thus relieving them from what might otherwise be their aridity and monotony, hyper-subtlety, and excess of hair splitting ingenuity and acuteness. The analysis, almost painfully minute and so continually recurring, of his "me" in all its fluctuations; the characterisation, trenchantly accurate and glitteringly brilliant, of the phenomena among which this "me" lives and moves and has its being; with here and there a touch of allegory or "symbol," and very occasionally a lyric strain subdued carefully by the employment of that invaluable pedal, humour: such are the chief literary ingredients of not only the latter and better part of *Sous l' Œil des Barbares*, but also of all M. Barrès' subsequent writings. A special point must here be made regarding M. Barrès' humour. Humour, as every one knows, is perhaps the rarest of literary qualities in France. M. Bourget (with whom one naturally is prompted to compare and contrast M. Barrès, as being to a certain extent the latter's prototype or forerunner) is deficient in humour, lamentably, as those would-be humourous touches in *Mensonges* and *Le Disciple* go to show. But that M. Barrès is possessed of the gift appears distinctly, if only from the chapter of the *Barbares* wherein the young "passionate pilgrim" seeking ever amidst the banality and baseness of the modern world the path which is to lead him to the recovery of some Holy Grail, encounters the spirit of successful mundane philosophy incarnate in the person of (impossible to doubt the malicious fidelity of the portraiture) no less an one than M. Ernest Renan. Like most other thinkers of this time, M. Barrès came early beneath the spell of M. Renân's exquisite intellectuality, and at first failed to distinguish the callous sensuality of his doctrines, so speciously disguised to represent a kind of refined and ornate Pyrrhonism; but the author of *Sous l' Œil des Barbares* would appear subsequently to have revolted, at least for a time, against such soullessness with a heartiness of antipathy almost worthy the *Spectator* newspaper itself. A charming, graceful girl (Worldly Pleasure or Success) has been stirring the young man's senses with her attractions. And now the old, stout, blue-eyed, bottle-nosed sophist—" M. X——, causeur divin, maître qui institua des doubles à toutes les certitudes, et dont le contact exquis amollit les plus rudes sectaires "—is represented as the material projection or ultimate philosophical expression of the damsel's " furtive " soul:—

> " He seems the shadow cast by this young girl's voluptuous image; the material appearance and shape of the furtive soul she signifies. His lips, disconcerting in the excess of their mobility, are like to this worldly creature's floating laugh; and, just as she enchants us by the undulations of her pliant frame, so does he overcome us all, through the perpetual approbativeness of his nodding poll."

A scene ensues which Aristophanes or Molière might have signed. In a parody, or rather a reproduction, exquisitely perfect, of the Renanesque mellifluence of speech, a series of precepts, maxims, axioms for the better guidance of the tyro through the world are formulated by the sensuous old sage, who meanwhile gradually but completely befuddles himself with glass upon glass of highly-sweetened absinthe, beneath the eye of a black-jacketed, white-aproned, frizzly-haired and side-whiskered Parisian waiter, with *serviette* tucked majestically under the left arm. Finally the listener feels his gorge rising at the flowery ignominiousness of the tun-bellied sophist's scheme, and—but M. Barrès must be left to relate the rest :—

> "The young man naïf, uncultured or provoked? failed to perceive the charms of this philosophy, and, impelled, as I suppose, by a perhaps hereditary feeling of respect for the categorical imperative, he transcended at one step the bounds of the Pyrrhonism that was being taught him; to the extent of suddenly bestowing upon this complex old person a thorough beating with his stick. The old man noisily expressed his affliction; but the other triumphantly exclaimed: '*Eh bien!* scratch the ironical, and you will find the elegiac.' He might even have replied with moral and metaphysical reasonings to the arguments of M. X——, if the waiters and the *maître d'hôtel* had not thrown them both out of doors.
>
> "*Et le peuple ricanait.*"

. . . One can imagine the scene with illustrations from the pencil of "Caran d'Ache." . . . No other satiric draughtsman of the day could accentuate so well the fantastic jocularity of the "symbol."

Further on in *Sous l'Œil des Barbares* our youth begins to intrigue with a view to social domination, for which, through his various graceful and attractive gifts, he is eminently well fitted, could he but stoop to devote the whole of his genius to the attainment of such an end. But here again is vexation, again deception, again discontent. . . . Always the quivering soul, the aching heart, the brain that grinds and grinds and grinds like the squirrel within its cage. . . .

At length, and if only for the purpose of getting a little further away from himself, he determines to put something of himself on paper. "He would copy strictly, without amplitude or ability" [his modesty leads M. Barrès to malign himself as regards this latter point] "the divers dreams which during the past five years had imprinted themselves upon his mind." And yet again, in this literary task he meets with naught but doubt, dissatisfaction, distress:—

> "Often, very often, wearied, bewildered by the monotony of his casuistry, overcome by the dread lest all the things he had ever known should be nothing more than puerile dreams, and still more discomposed at the thought of resuming a genuine, firm, earnest, useful life, he would stop short. . . ."

And the Book—this little particularising, ratiocinating record of the restless wanderings of a superior soul in quest of its appropriate sphere—terminates despairingly with the cry:—

> "O master, master, where art thou, whom I long to love, to serve, to whom I commit myself!
>
> "Thee alone, O master, if somewhere thou hast existence, be thou axiom, religion, or prince of men."

II.

A preponderant share of space has been accorded to the consideration of *Sous l'Œil des Barbares*. Comments upon its companion volumes, *Un Homme Libre* and *Le Jardin de Bérénice*, shall not, and need not, be extended to any such lengths. We have seen now nearly as much of M. Barrès as even his writings could be expected to reveal. Consequently only the briefest mention will be made of the more salient distinctive features differentiating his two later books from the first one.

In *Un Homme Libre* M. Barrès is found to have advanced several steps further towards the wished-for goal of complete practical possession and domination of Self. His philosophy, which in the *Barbares* floated at random like the *tour-*

billons or *atômes crochus* of French metaphysicians of the classic age, now has crystallized itself, so to speak, and taken a definite form to its substance. The sole actual reality is Self; for what more is the whole exterior universe than the projection of Self upon the Infinite? In Self, therefore, in Self and for Self, must we resignedly elect to live. Nor must we hope for any actual felicity, either present or to come; but must seek and find, in simply the daily incidents of our hopeless quest, sufficient interest and entertainment to keep us passively content:—

> " Continually to seek for peace and happiness, with the conviction that we never shall find them, is the solution I propose. We must make our pleasure consist in the experiments we undertake, and not in the results which these experiments may seem to offer. Let us amuse ourselves with the means, and have no thought for the end. Thus shall we escape from the feelings of unrest that overtook those too high-minded children " [The author, in a manner most characteristic of his mind and method, is here considering the lamentable case of so many young children who, of late years, not in France only, but in other countries, have sought a refuge from life in the arms of voluntary death.] "and which were solely due to the disproportion between the objects they aspired to and those which they attained."

Whereas *Sous l'Œil des Barbares* was written in the third person, *Un Homme Libre* is couched in the form of a diary. It relates the metaphysical experiments and experiences of the author in the company of his "ami Simon," a personage very quaintly but felicitously presented in somewhat the tone and style of *Tristam Shandy*, for example. The author's "friend Simon" and he, disgusted, each in his own peculiar way, with the general inanity and vulgarity of people and things, go off to play together at being hermits in an isolated provincial retreat, where day after day they remain, sounding the inmost recesses of their minds and souls, comparing notes and discussing results. The two recluses, from morning to night, and often from night to morning, think, and converse, and read; read, more particularly, the works of such morbidly acute self-analysts as the Saint-Beuve of the *première manière* and as Benjamin Constant in his autobiographical *Adolphe;* Balzac and the other writers of action being discarded as too "disturbing." And these readings provide M. Barrès with an opportunity for some criticism of the picturesque, intimate, searchingly psychological type, so fine in its penetration, and in its literary flavour so delightful, that I would willingly rest his reputation upon these chapters alone. The method of M. Barrès as a critic is to discover and describe himself in and through the writers whom he examines. This, in the last analysis, is the only true criticism, as every true critic, if he is frank enough, must fain admit.

A further interesting and prominent feature in the pages of *Un Homme Libre* is the compendious and artistically elaborated account of, as it were, the soul-life from century to century of M. Barrès' native province, Lorraine: a perfect monograph and minor masterpiece in its way; but here again, for excellent artistic reasons, excerpts are not to be essayed.

Before the volume is half over the hero and his "ami Simon" fall apart, and their hermit life of "Saint Germain" is at an end. Simon returns to the more active career for which he is naturally fitted, and the other drifts off alone into the principal towns of Italy, there to tread still the mill of introspection, and to grasp daily, hourly, at divine but elusive shadows which the contemplation of the purest triumphs of art calls forth "not as single spies, but in battalions." A sentimental episode (somewhat materially sentimental) supervenes . . . Its ultimate result is to revive a sense of the vanity of all things, and more especially the things of the flesh; and, at the close of *Un Homme Libre*, the experimentalist, whilst yet allowing his mere body to go on living in the midst of men, retreats for good and all into the penetralia of his mind as into an impregnable, inaccessible fortress, where he no longer shall find himself "beneath the eye of barbarians," but will be able to exist as a "freeman," at last and indeed;—

"I now live within a dream, composed of moral elegance and of accuracy of vision. Even vulgarity cannot disturb me, for, seated in the heart of my lucid palace, I drown the scandalous murmurs arising towards me from the outer horde by means of the varied *arias* my soul can play to me at will.

"Solitude I have renounced; I have decided to erect my tent in the midst of the living age, because of certain appetites which can find a vent only in active life. In isolation they disturbed my quiet, like so many mercenaries out of employ. The baser part of my being, ill content with inaction, at times would interfere with what is best in me. I have come down among men in order to procure for it playthings, so that henceforward it may leave me in peace.

* * * *

Alienus! Foreign to the exterior world, foreign even to my past, foreign to my very instincts. . . . . . . truly I am an *Homme Libre!*"

III.

Le Jardin de Bérénice, quite recently brought out, and hailed from the moment it appeared with the admiring comments of Paul Bourget,

Jules Lemaître, Anatole France, and all the other leading literary critics of the hour in France, marks, as was to be expected, a still later stage in the intellectual and spiritual development of M. Barrès. In the interval between the production of *Un Homme Libre* and of this *Bérénice*, third and last panel of the "triptych," or portion of the "trilogy," our experimentalist has been inoculating himself carefully with a desire for public life. As a practical result, he has caused himself to be elected a deputy for Nancy, the capital of his province, and now M. Barrès sits as one of the youngest members of the Corps Législatif. Under a slightly modified form ("Tout est vrai là-dedans, rien n'y est exact," the author says at the close) *Le Jardin de Bérénice* is the narrative of his real electoral experiences and impressions, adorned with and complicated by incidents introducing a species of Aspasia in little, a creature imbued with the greatest delicacy and charm, albeit touched, through the irresistible effect of corrupting circumstances, with that taint which from the first overshadows, as a standing menace, all natures at once so fine and so complex, and which only the most favourable, most fortunate conditions can have power definitely to avert and prevent. Life is hard—to such as these more particularly—and vice, how terribly strong! The wise and good will pity, pardon, deplore; only the naturally bad and base will think to blame or to condemn.

When Philippe (as the hero, in this last volume, is finally christened, by way of concession, says M. Barrès, with a graceful airy impertinence all his own, to the wishes of certain amiable lady readers) first encounters, in the South of France, whither he has gone to conduct his electoral campaign, Bérénice grown into a lovely woman, she appears to him "attired in weeds, and delicately voluptuous of countenance." She is living in a villa near the town, and lamenting the loss of a former lover whom she, unusually enough, herself had sincerely loved. Years before, Philippe had known her in Paris, as a precociously perverted child, a dancing girl at one of the principal theatres. "Elle eut plus de défaillances qu'aucune personne de son âge," says the writer, but as in Shakespeare's Cleopatra: "Vilest things become themselves in her." Hers was the privilege divine, to make a very fault appear a beauty:—

"I saw her once
Hop forty paces through the public street;
And, having lost her breath, she spoke, and panted,
That she did make defect, perfection,
And, breathless, power breathe forth."

"Always," the author adds, in a phrase of delicious gentleness and beauty, "it was with tenderness of look and word that she transgressed; and upon that little hand, after so many dreadful things, I yet can behold no sin." And then he speaks of the peculiar coldness of her little visage, on which the intensity of her native sensibilities appeared, as it were, to be frozen stiff and hard:—

"That coldness beneath which I could divine such fearful readiness to feel . . . *Masque entêté de jeune reine aux cheveux plats!* Never were eyes so grave, nor so well able to discern the bitterness ever bubbling at the root of things . . . Proud as they are, little beings of this description can love those only who appeal to their imagination. They go from the princes of the earth to the worst of outlaws. Not admitted to be the adulating mistress of a king, such women become rebels, whose acrid downtrodden beauty pains the observer's soul."

Bérénice is being courted by a young man of the town, in whom Philippe sees the incarnation of aggressive mediocrity and materialism, and whom he dubs "l'Adversaire" in consequence. This "Adversary," through the effects of Philippe's highly disinterested but somewhat ill-judged advice, finally marries Bérénice, who shortly afterwards dies; Phillippe's candidature is successful, and he now determines to cultivate an interest in the people, among whom alone, they being "unconscious," may still exist some germ of future good. With regard to himself, he resolves, in the name and for the sake of his further intellectual "freedom," to seek systematically what he terms "a considerable material independency." Thus, apparently, M. Barrès no longer would inflict on M. Renan the figurative caning of *Sous l'Œil des Barbares;* and, perhaps, they are not quite wrong, the people in Paris who are just now applying the nickname of "Miss Renan" to the young author of *Le Jardin de Bérénice*, as Alfred de Musset in his time was styled "Mademoiselle Byron:" for is not the following passage, with which *Le Jardin de Bérénice* concludes, almost exactly in the spirit of the teachings of the mellifluous sage?

"Money: such is the refuge wherein minds anxious for the integrity of their inner life will best be able to await the organising of some institution analogous to the religious orders which, spontaneously arising in consequence of that same oppression of the 'me' described in *Sous l'Œil des Barbares*, were the places where formerly were elaborated practical rules for becoming *Un Homme Libre*, and where arose that admirable vision of the heavenly spirit at work amidst the world which, under the more modern name of the 'unconscious,' Philippe discovered in the *Jardin de Bérénice*."

The pretext here advanced in language which my translation so regrettably impairs, is lofty. . . Nevertheless, it appears that *l'argent* is the last word of M. Maurice Barrès' latest book. The elegiac poet, the "ironist," the stylist, the casuist and metaphysician, comes in the last resort to look on *l'argent* as the thing most necessary to possess and best worth the trouble to acquire. Herein, some may think, is involved a base surrender to the Zeitgeist; but I for my part fail to perceive why that which would be considered a highly commendable ambition in a pork-butcher, should by anyone be deemed a dishonourable inclination on the part of one of the most delicate, distinguished, original, ardent, and naturally aristocratic individualities of this time. What amount of self-seeking, or even money-seeking, definitively could overcome or outweigh the innate nobility of the author of *Sous l'Œil des Barbares*, *Un Homme Libre*, and *Le Jardine de Bérénice?* If, indeed, rewards of writing were according to the degree of merit in the writer, it is certain that *l'argent* would come of its own accord to M. Maurice Barrès and without any further ado.

And yet—and yet the sadness of it: the dreams, the longings, the noble fever, the ceaseless, ardent, anxious search, all settling down at last into the numb materialism of this renouncement! The blame?—where lies it, if not with Life itself and Life's unbearable conditions.